A Love REKINDLED

Jordan Smith

ISBN 978-1-63630-431-1 (Paperback)
ISBN 978-1-63630-432-8 (Digital)

Covenant Books, Inc.
11661 Hwy 707
Murrells Inlet, SC 29576
www.covenantbooks.com

To my papaw—I will see you in the morning.

1

Oneʼs life is a rollercoaster; sometimes you are on top of the world, whereas others, you are in a bottomless pit. The two are intertwined, and it is impossible to live a life worth living without experiencing both. At times, the lows may seem to occur more than the highs and may seem unbearable. This is where we learn to lean on God and not our own selves.

*****

"Welcome, class, to Physical Chemistry 1," Professor Salyers announced to the room full of students. "Throughout this semester, you will not only be learning the art of thermodynamics in a classroom setting but will also be engaging in a variety of laboratory techniques. I promise to try and make this a fun class, as you can clearly see from the doughnuts that I brought this morning." Both the professor and the group of students chuckled lightly. "Iʼm not going to lie; this will be a difficult class, but I promise that we will get through it together."

After reviewing the lengthy syllabus for the class, the young professor barely had enough time to begin reviewing chapter 1 of the textbook before class came to an end.

"Please finish reading chapter 1, and we will go more in depth on Wednesday," he announced to the students as they grabbed their backpacks and left the room, embarking on their journeys to their following classes.

As the classroom emptied, nineteen-year-old Emma grabbed her backpack as well and caught up with her closest friend and roommate, Angela.

"So how do you think the semester will go?" Angela asked Emma on their way out. "The assignments don't sound terribly bad, but I am definitely worried about the course content."

"I don't think it'll be as hard as you think," Emma replied.

"Easy for you to say; you're a natural."

Now, Emma was by no means a natural in her studies, but she had learned that hard work and dedication were the keys to success. Sometimes, she would only sleep a few hours a night; other times, she wouldn't sleep a wink. However, she had found a system that somehow worked for her.

"If you would just sit still for a few hours and study, maybe you wouldn't be so worried about the class," Emma teased.

"You know me, Em. I need a good party thrown in the mix. Speaking of, there is a party tonight—"

"No, thanks."

"And you are coming with me. No homework yet, no excuses."

"We were just assigned homework five minutes ago."

"Yeah, but that's just reading and doesn't count. I'll look like a fool if I go alone. Please…"

"Okay, fine. I'll go; just calm down, Ang."

"Don't worry about that; I'm already feeling my worries fade away," she said, swaying back and forth. "What else do you have on your schedule for today?"

"Only English literature and positive psychology."

"Well, I am *positive* that you will excel at both. See what I did there? Positive? I crack myself up."

"Yeah, Ang. You're a real comedian all right," Emma laughed, rolling her eyes. "I'll catch up with you later."

After classes had finished for the afternoon, Emma and Angela began to dress for the Luau-themed party. Angela donned a short tight-fitted yellow dress, accompanied by a pair of six-inch heels. Her blond curls cascaded down her back, and she looked as if she was an angel in disguise. Emma, on the other hand, had decided to dress in a more modest fashion. She wore a long flowing dress covered in flower print. Despite Angela's protests, she also wore a light sweater and flats.

"Can you just dress up for once, Emma?" Angela pleaded.

"What are you talking about? I am dressed up! I'm wearing a dress, just in case you hadn't noticed."

"I mean, let loose a little. Show off your natural curves." She shimmied.

Emma crossed her arms to stand her ground.

"At least take off the sweater and put on some heels." She looked at Emma sternly. "And I promise to help you study this weekend."

Emma thought for a moment. "Fine, I suppose that's a compromise that I can live with."

"Thank goodness," Angela said, reaching into her closet to find a pair of heels.

"A pair that I can wear, preferably without falling, please."

"So not these, then?" She held up heels higher than her own.

"Maybe a tad smaller."

"How about these?" She held up a pair of heels almost identical to the ones she was wearing.

"Well, if that's the only pair, then…"

"Perfect, slip them on, and let me fix your hair."

"What's wrong with my hair?" Emma frowned.

"Nothing, I just really want to curl those brown locks."

"Ang, we're going to be late meeting the others. I promise that you can curl it next time."

"Okay," she said in a disappointed tone, looking down. When she raised her head, she looked back at Emma. "Wow, Em. You look like some kind of Grecian goddess. I'll have to try and keep all the boys off you tonight." She winked.

"Ang…I'm only going for a few minutes and then come back here. I already have a paper that I need to begin working on, as well as—"

"Okay," Angela interrupted. "I understand, but I can stay as long as I want, right?"

"Right," Emma laughed. "Just don't do anything too crazy."

"Em, have you met me? Crazy is my middle name. Now, let's go."

On their way to the party, Emma and Angela met up with their other friends, Sara, Thomas, and Gerald. Sara was a philosophy major, whereas Thomas and Gerald favored the sciences like Emma and Angela. Thomas enjoyed engineering, and Gerald enjoyed zoology. The group had been close friends since freshman year, and their friendship had only grown stronger over the years.

Emma noticed that Sara had also dressed more modest.

"Hey, girls!" Sara said, running up and throwing her arms around Emma. "How was your summer? I missed us all hanging out together!"

"It was a pretty good time off," Emma replied. "I mostly read and took advantage of sleeping in. Nothing too exciting. How about you? Anything fun?"

"Girl, you know it! I went to party after party."

Emma raised an eyebrow.

"Just kidding," she giggled. "I mostly stayed an introvert except for family time…as usual."

"Shew, I thought for a minute that Ang was rubbing off on you!"

"Hey!" Angela smacked Emma lightly. "I'm standing right here and do take offense to that!"

The group burst out laughing.

"Come on, guys! Am I really the only exciting person in this group?"

"No fair!" Thomas and Gerald replied in unison.

"Yeah, you never asked about us and our summers!" Gerald said defensively.

"All right then," Angela said smugly, luring the two into her trap, "what have you boys done?"

Thomas and Gerald looked at each other and then down at their shoes.

"Come on, Gerald," Thomas said. "She asked you a question."

"By all means, go ahead," Gerald responded.

"You two didn't actually do anything exciting, did you?" Angela stated more than asked.

The boys looked at each other sheepishly.

"Oh!" Thomas exclaimed. "We have made a new friend!"

"Yeah," Gerald joined in. "He's meeting us at the party."

"And who is this mystery guy? He is real, right?" Angela inquired as the group finally reached the party.

"Of course, he's real. Here he is now."

Just then, Emma stopped in her tracks as she saw a familiar figure walking toward them. He was muscular and tall with a mess of brown hair; Emma would have known him anywhere.

"Nicholas?" Emma asked, shocked.

The boy's head shot toward her. "Emma? What are you doing here?"

"What am I doing? I attend school here. What are you—I thought you went back to England."

"I did, but I convinced my parents to allow me to study in the States, and a good thing I did. I didn't think that I would ever see you again. You look just…wow." He gave her a good look over.

Emma blushed, and he took a step closer to where they were less than a foot apart.

"Hello!" Angela interjected, and the two slowly stepped apart. "Can someone please tell me what is going on? I'm guessing that you two know each other already?"

"Sorry," Emma apologized. "Yes, we were friends through most of high school until senior year, when his family left for England."

"We weren't just friends," Nicholas said. "Em and I were best friends, and I've never met a friend like her since. Kind and loyal. Someone that you can tell anything to." He looked at Emma knowingly, and she began to blush yet again.

"Well, Nicky boy," Thomas said, patting him on the back, clearly oblivious to the long-awaited reunion. "Are you ready to party?"

"Sure, but it's Nicholas, if you don't mind." He laughed.

"All right, guys," Gerald said, bouncing up and down. "Let's go, let's go, let's go!"

"How much caffeine is he on?" Nicholas asked curiously.

"None, actually," Sara giggled. "He's just naturally... enthusiastic."

"You all go ahead," Angela said. "Emma and I will catch up in a minute."

As the group dispersed into the crowd, Angela grabbed onto Emma's arm. "Only friends?" Angela asked. "You have got to be kidding me. He's adorable and has that amazing accent. You two were seriously nothing more than friends?"

Now, Emma enjoyed a nice British accent as well as the next girl. She could probably listen to the melodious sound all day, but the two had only ever been friends, and this she swore to Angela.

"Well..." Angela said, thinking a moment, "I believe you."

"Thank you—"

"But," she interrupted, "I am officially rooting for you two as a couple."

"What? You're what?"

"There's obviously some sparks flying around between you two, and I can see them. I am betting that at least by the end of the school year, you will be together like in famous romance novels, if not sooner." Angela was matter-of-fact, and once she set her mind to something, she saw it through.

Emma couldn't help but laugh. "I'm sorry to tell you but you're wrong. No sparks. Nothing. We were only friends, and that's all we're ever going to be. Trust me."

"We'll see," Angela said. "I'm also going to go out on a limb and say that you're probably staying for more than a few minutes tonight...because of a certain someone."

"I might stay for half an hour at the most."

"Sure," she said, rolling her eyes. "I bet that you'll stay the entire night, and possibly a bit longer."

Angela, of course, turned out to be right. Emma stayed much longer than her half an hour. She and Nicholas had spoken all night at the party, never missing a beat. They had discussed mainly his time in England and the sightseeing he had done when he had visited the rest of Europe.

At one point, the fraternity party played a slower song, and Angela had pushed the two together on the dance floor.

"Just like old times," Nicholas said, gently grabbing one of Emma's hands and placing the other on her waist.

Emma smiled and placed her free hand on his shoulder. "So do you enjoy being back in the States?"

"I enjoy being back with you," Nicholas said with a sly smirk.

Emma turned scarlet and could feel the heat being emitted from her cheeks. There was just something about being around him. He could make her feel calm yet excited at the same time.

"I missed you too," she replied teasingly. "But really, what do you think so far about the campus?"

"For starters, you're changing the conversation, but I'll allow that to pass this once." An eyebrow raised. "The campus itself is beautiful," Nicholas said, looking into her eyes intensely. Emma looked down as he continued, "The library is wonderful, but I think the science building, Rowan, I believe, is the nicest of them all. Perfect for my biology major."

"Really?" Emma asked.

"Yeah, why?"

"I'm a chemistry major. We'll be in the same building for most classes. This will be so exciting!"

Nicholas's eyes gleamed, and he gave Emma a small twirl.

The two friends danced for the rest of the night, reliving the old days, excited for the ones ahead.

2

As Emma tossed and turned in her sleep that night, she kept reliving flashbacks of her time spent with Nicholas.

*****

A cool breeze flew over the warm summer air, and butterflies were fluttering among the flowers. Emma found herself in a soft white sundress sitting on a blanket next to a picnic basket. Across from her was her close friend Nicholas.

"Wait until you see what I packed for us, Em." He proceeded to pull out a basket of berries, a variety of cheeses, and two bottles of his mother's homemade lemonade.

"Oh my, Nicholas. It all looks so wonderful. Thank you again for doing this."

"I'm glad you like it," he said, biting into a strawberry.

"Is there some kind of special occasion that I don't know about?" Emma asked.

"No, just a…thank you lunch," he said hesitantly.

"Thank you? For what?" She gave a confused look.

"For being my friend, that's all." He smiled sweetly.

"Nicholas, is everything okay?"

"Of course. By the way," he said, quickly changing the topic, "this lemonade is Mom's best yet."

Emma knew deep down that something was off, but she decided to drop the subject. She had a feeling that Nicholas would tell her in time what exactly was going on.

After the two friends finished eating, they laid back on the picnic blanket. Emma could feel the brush of soft grass against her bare feet. A few moments of silence passed.

Nicholas's head turned to look at Emma. "What are your desires, Em?" he asked quietly.

Now, this was no strange question to Emma as the two always shared in deep, intellectual, theological discussions. However, the tone of his voice this time was different, but she wasn't sure why.

"I suppose that I want what most people do. Grow up, marry, start a family, and live a life worth living."

"That's what you want. What everyone wants. But, Emma, what do *you* personally desire?"

Emma pondered for a few minutes as she searched her soul. What exactly did she desire?

"I desire a closer relationship with Jesus," she finally said. "Mine now has been faltering, and I've only been praising Him when good things happen in my life. I need to learn to praise Him in the bad times as well. I desire to draw closer to Him, and I pray that He will surround me with people who will help me draw closer to Him."

"I, too, desire that, Emma. I need to learn to seek God first and put Him first in all things. It's rather difficult when you become so busy; He tends to be put on the back burner. He wants us to come to Him for everything. God desires a relationship with us, and we should desire a relationship with Him."

Emma closed her eyes and allowed the sun to soak into her chilled skin. She always ended up with goosebumps when speaking on topics such as this. The Holy Spirit would never fail to fill the air. Like the Bible says, "Where two or more are gathered together, there is the presence of God." She could definitely feel Him there.

"Emma?" His voice was soft, softer than Emma had heard from him before.

"Yes, Nicholas?"

"There's something else I need to tell you. I really don't want to because I don't want it to become reality."

This was the reason for the thank you picnic; she knew that something had been off.

As Emma opened her eyes to look at his, she noticed that he was worked up. She absentmindedly grabbed his hand to calm him and asked what was wrong.

"I'm…leaving," he said with a twinge of pain in his voice, and his hand gripped tight to hers. It was as if he wouldn't have to leave if he held hard enough.

Emma withstood the slight pain and began her questioning. "Leaving? What do you mean?" She asked calmly, soothingly.

"Emma…my family and I are moving back to England."

She was in complete shock. How could he be leaving her? She did have other friends, but none were like him. However, she had to stay composed for his sake, as well as hers.

"When?" she asked quietly, looking down. She began picking at a piece of grass that had blown onto their blanket.

"Tomorrow morning." Nicholas looked in the same direction, sorrow in his voice.

"So soon?"

"I'm afraid so. I've wanted to tell you for a while, but it never seemed to be the right time."

Silence passed between the two.

"I hope you find friends plentiful and happiness wherever you are," Emma barely whispered.

"Emma, I don't want to hurt you at all—"

"I'm not hurt," she said, raising her head. "I sincerely wish you happiness, all in the world." She tried a sweet false smile but was heartbroken on the inside.

Why was he leaving? How could he be leaving? The two had become so close these past couple of years to the point that they were almost inseparable. But now, now all that was for naught.

"We can still keep in touch," Nicholas said, with glistening eyes, almost reading her mind.

"Of course."

Another moment of silence passed.

"Emma," Nicholas whispered, "my second desire is to stay here with you."

She blushed bright red. Surely, he couldn't mean that.

Before she could dwell anymore on this surprising revelation, Emma's dream came to an end.

A few years had passed since Nicholas had left for England. Since that time, she had graduated high school and began college. Her life was going well, excellent even. She had made numerous friends and was excelling in her courses. Because of this, she only occasionally thought of Nicholas; and when she did, she felt both sadness and guilt.

The beginning of his absence had been hard on her—she had lost her closest ally. However, the two messaged constantly, almost every day. As time passed, the messages became scarcer, on both accounts. Emma would sometimes initiate the conversation but chose to do so rarely for fear of bothering Nicholas. This is what had happened to their relationship: best friends turned to mere acquaintances. However, Emma tended not to dwell too much on this if she could help it. She had her best friend, Angela, and her other close friends, Sara, Thomas, and Gerald. But what was happening now? Was Nicholas really back, or was this just another wonderful dream of hers that her subconscious had concocted for her?

*****

Emma lay in bed that morning as her first class of the day did not begin until after lunch. She replayed the previous night in her head over and over until Angela arose. As soon as she noticed that Emma was wide awake, she rushed over and lightly jumped up on her bed.

"So..." she began.

"So..." Emma mimicked.

"I saw some sparks flying last night, and it was magical. I think that we are on track to have you a relationship before the end of the school year, maybe even before the end of the semester."

"Ang, Nicholas and I don't feel that way about each other. We're just friends."

"Em, you might not see it now, but the way he looked at you... he definitely is interested in being more than friends."

Emma blushed and tossed a pillow at Angela, who quickly ducked.

"You know I'm right," she continued. "I know that you feel something for him too! This romance novel is going to write itself!"

"You're right. I do feel something for him."

"Aha!"

"Yeah, it's called friendship, Angela!"

She simply rolled her eyes at Emma. "You may think right now that it's just a friendship, but just you wait. Pay attention to him the next time you see him, and you'll see *the look*."

"What's *the look*?" Emma asked curiously.

"You have to experience it firsthand to understand the full effect; but it's pretty much saying that he wants you, loves you, and has to be with you. It's a longing look of passion." She looked off into the distance as she spoke.

"Earth to Angela." Emma waved her hand in front of Angela's face, and she whipped back to reality. "When are you going to give up on this notion that Nicholas and I are more than friends?"

"When you *both* tell me with a blank look on your faces, look me in the eyes without blushing or smiling, or tell me that you only want to be friends."

The heat began to rise to Emma's cheeks, but she wasn't sure why. She quickly looked away.

"See? Just thinking about him and you're already blushing," she said teasingly.

"I am not!" she denied but blushed even more. Her hands involuntarily reached up to her face, and she felt the heat from her cheeks.

"Face it, girl. You're falling, and you're falling hard."

3

Saturday morning, Emma, Angela, and Sara decided to head to Rowan Science Center to study. Although the library was closer to their dormitory, Rowan was much more comfortable. Large tables were accompanied by leather chairs. White boards filled the hallways.

As Emma walked into the building, she immediately knew she was going to have a great day. She breathed in deeply the scent of newly cleaned tables combined with that of old textbooks. She was so happy to be back to her home away from home.

The three girls decided to set up their studies in the main lobby. As usual, it was the perfect setting. One wall had been constructed to be completely windows, which made for a beautiful view on any kind of day. The other was filled with white boards, which helped tremendously when trying to study.

Emma sat in a chair with an ottoman, pulled out her physical chemistry book, and began her homework. Approximately half an hour into their studies, a familiar voice rang through the air.

"What's going on, ladies?" Gerald asked, walking up to the group.

"Nothing too exciting," Sara replied smiling. "Just studying."

"Well, Nicholas, Thomas, and I are meeting up with some of the guys. When they arrive, will you let them know that we are just down the hall to the right?"

"Sure will!" Sara said a bit too enthusiastically. "I mean, no problem."

"Thanks," Gerald said before turning to leave.

After he was well out of hearing distance, both Emma and Angela turned to look at Sara.

"Girl," Angela began, "What was that?"

"What was what?" Sara asked innocently.

"You know exactly what we're talking about," Emma answered.

Sara shot a look toward the ground. "Fine, fine. I may sort of… like…Gerald," she muttered.

The other two girls squealed quietly with excitement.

"It's not a big deal. He probably doesn't even like me back. At least, not like that." She sighed deeply and allowed her low self-esteem to fill her head with negative thoughts.

"How could he not?" Emma asked. "You're beautiful, inside and out, caring, intelligent, and talented at so many things. The list could go on and on."

"Thanks, Em," Sara said, looking back up toward the girls. "I hope that one day I'll know if all of those qualities are enough."

"What do you mean?" Angela asked.

"Well, I've been in love so many times before. The beginning is always so wonderful, but I've been scorned each time. I've been told over and over again that I'm just not good enough." Her eyes began to water.

"Don't listen to any of those people," Emma said. "If they truly loved you, they would have never said those things or even thought them. God has someone special out there for you. You may or may not have met him yet, but when you begin the relationship and keep God at the center, you'll know what He had in store for you the whole time."

"And Gerald isn't like those people," Angela said. "We all know him to be kind and honest; he's a great catch."

"Thanks, guys," Sara said, tears still staining her eyes. "I love you both like sisters."

The three girls hugged, and as the embrace ended, Thomas and Nicholas strolled up to the group.

"We're meeting up with Gerald," Thomas said cautiously. "Is everything okay?"

"Yeah, just a little worried over an upcoming presentation," Angela lied smoothly. "He's down the hall on the right."

"Okay then, if you're sure everything's all right..." Thomas said as he walked off.

"Ladies," Nicholas winked subtly at Emma, and then he, too, was gone.

Angela arched an eyebrow at Emma, who simply rolled her eyes. The interaction happened in a flash, too quick for Sara to even notice.

After a few more hours of studying, Angela and Sara decided to be done for the day. They begged Emma to go shopping with them, but she refused, stating that her homework was more important. After a lengthy discussion about how Emma studied too much, the girls left, promising to come back and grab her for dinner.

Emma looked around and noticed that the lobby was now empty. She listened but heard no large groups in the hallway. She decided to move to a large circular table where she could spread out her textbooks, notebooks, and whatever else she needed.

Emma was nose-deep in her studies when she both heard and felt a large thud hit the table. She involuntarily jumped in her seat.

"Sorry for the scare, but do you mind terribly if I join you?" Nicholas asked, pulling up a chair.

"Sure," Emma said, not understanding why heat began flooding her cheeks.

As Nicholas unpacked his bag, she was able to pay him more notice. He had grown taller and more muscular since high school. She noticed the latter in particular as he rolled his dress shirt sleeves to his elbows. She blushed again and continued her studies.

For the next hour, the two worked in perfect harmony. Emma continued her note-taking while Nicholas worked his equations. After several trips to the whiteboard, he placed his head in his hands.

"Everything okay?" Emma asked.

"I don't understand what I'm doing wrong with this chemistry problem, Em." He brushed his fingers through his hair. "Can you look over it for me?"

Emma walked up to the whiteboard and grabbed a marker. "I see," she said, motioning after a few minutes for Nicholas to join her. "You need to convert from grams to kilograms. Right here." She circled the error.

"Oh," he said with understanding and a bit of relief. "I've been working this problem forever. Thanks!"

As he reached for the marker, their fingers lightly brushed. Both hands stopped, and the two looked at each other. Nicholas's deep blue eyes focused solely on Emma as if searching her soul. Emma smiled softly before glancing away from the intense stare. She felt her heart speed up but was not sure as to the reason.

"I had better go ahead and fix this," Nicholas said quietly, but he did not return to his work. Instead, he glanced at Emma, his stare unwavering.

Emma felt his stare and turned back, asking if everything was okay.

"It's just…I've missed hanging out with you, just one on one, and it feels…right." He leaned a tad closer until they were merely inches apart.

Emma met his stare, but this time, she did not look away. It felt as if hours had passed until their mutual gaze was finally broken by Angela's presence. She had waltzed into the room without interrupting their longing glances.

"Umm…Emma," she slowly began, "I came to grab you for dinner…unless I'm interrupting something."

"No, no," Emma started, ever so slightly stepping away from Nicholas. "Nothing's being interrupted."

"Just some chemistry," Nicholas smirked.

"Yes, chemistry," Emma sighed with relief. "Homework. Chemistry homework," she corrected.

"Well, like I said, Em, just coming to grab you for dinner. Would you like to join us, Nicholas?"

"No, thanks. I think I'll stick around here for a bit, finishing up these problems."

After Emma had gathered her belongings, the girls said their goodbyes and left. When they had fully exited the building, Angela whirled around. "What was *that*?"

"What was what?" Emma asked, confused.

"I walked into some kind of Jane Austen novel. You two were gazing into each other's eyes full of longing and desire. You didn't even acknowledge me until I spoke. Do you even know how long I had been standing there?"

Emma pondered for a few seconds. "To be honest, no, but I have a perfectly reasonable explanation."

"Which is?" Angela asked, placing a hand on her hip.

"I have no idea," she said with honesty.

"Well, I have your explanation for you. You both are totally flirting with each other!"'

"But I don't know how to flirt, Ang." Emma's tone was matter-of-fact.

"Well, Nicholas certainly does," she said, giggling.

"He was not!"

"Girl, are you blind? Who just stares into someone else's eyes, oblivious to the surrounding world? Who says sweet words and then gives you a smirk? Someone who is interested, and Nicholas is definitely interested in you!"

"*Me?*"

"Yes, *you*. Do you even realize how close you two were standing when I walked in? So close that I was rooting for a kiss."

"Angela," Emma shushed, "you can't walk around saying things like that."

"Even if it's true?"

"Well, it's not true and will never be true," she said defensively.

Angela shook her head. "Open up your heart, Em, and you'll see what I've been talking about."

Emma took some time to process her accusations. Why would someone like Nicholas be interested in her? This clearly must be a misunderstanding on Angela's part, but why then would she have been so easily flustered tonight? And did she literally feel electricity when their hands touched? No, it couldn't be. It simply couldn't be.

The rest of the night, Emma pondered on these questions and on her own feelings with which she had not fully come to terms.

4

Emma was extremely excited when Wednesday night came because it was the first campus worship session of the semester. This was the first year where she was in charge, well, kind of in charge. She shared the role with two other friends because three coordinators were required for such a large event. The service took place every Wednesday regardless of the weather conditions outside. Each week, local churches would take turns sponsoring the event, bringing food, as well as the message. Altogether, including setup and cleanup, the event lasted three hours. Despite how much homework Emma had, she always made time for this.

A social had been given the week prior, requesting that people come if able, and this had definitely paid off. A dozen people had already showed up before the room had been set up and the food brought. Emma was asked by the other two leads to welcome everyone while they finished setting up the chairs. Even though Emma did not converse easily with strangers, she took her position very seriously and headed out the door into the crowd. As she exited the room, she noticed a girl standing alone, clutching at her Bible. Emma decided to approach her first.

"Hello, I'm Emma, one of the leads here. Thank you so much for coming!" She outstretched her hand.

The girl took the handshake. "Nice to meet you. I'm Brittany." The girl possessed the most angelic features she had seen before on anyone. Not only that, her voice also had a musical intonation.

"Nice to meet you as well," Emma replied. "How are you enjoying school so far?"

"This is my first year here, and to be honest, I was really nervous at the beginning. Everyone is so nice though, especially the professors."

"That's so nice to hear! What are you majoring in?"

"Sociology with a minor in philosophy."

"I'll have to introduce you to my friend Sara. She's also studying philosophy."

The two girls spoke for a few more minutes until Emma thought it was time to take her leave in order to introduce herself to the others. She met some friendly new faces, mostly freshmen, who were excited for the worship service. Others in the crowd were regulars, coming every week last year. Eventually, Sara and Gerald arrived to run through the music set before the service.

"I'm sorry that we're late! We've been trying to get the computer up and running, but the program's frozen," Gerald, the one in charge of projection, said. "Sara can lead the singing, but we won't have any lyrics on the screen."

"Let me think a minute," Emma said, puzzled. "What songs are you all singing tonight?"

Sara and Gerald listed off the names.

"Give me the lyrics, and I'll run downstairs and make some copies to pass out. We can do it the old-fashioned way."

Emma took the songbook and headed downstairs to the lobby. As she was typing in her password to the computer, Nicholas strolled up.

"Hey, Emma. What's going on? Shouldn't you be upstairs?" He slightly tipped his head to the side.

"I would be, but I need to print off copies of these lyrics. Our computer system is frozen, so we can't project anything tonight."

"Before you make those copies, let me take a look at it."

The two quickly headed back upstairs.

"Hey, Gerald. Let Nicholas look at the computer. He thinks that he may be able to fix it."

Gerald gladly handed over the machine. "I don't know, man. I can't figure out what's wrong. It's normally fine."

"Give me a minute, and I'll see what I can do," Nicholas replied.

After running what seemed like a few diagnostics, he had the computer back up and running, even already connected to the projector.

"Woah," Gerald said in awe. "Thanks, man." He patted Nicholas on the back and walked off to begin music practice.

"That was amazing, Nicholas," Emma exclaimed. "How did you do that?"

"The computer just needed to be turned off and back on, but don't let Gerald find out."

Emma chuckled. "I can't believe that it was that easy."

About that time, the doors were opened to all the students to enter the meeting place. Emma was a little worried as she would be speaking to the crowd first. As each individual trickled in, Emma's heart beat faster and faster. Nicholas took notice of this and lightly squeezed her hand. A silent "You've got this." She took one last deep breath and walked to the front of the room.

"Thank you all so much for coming to campus worship tonight! I'd just like to say, on behalf of our team, that we are extremely excited to have you here. Let me share a little bit about myself. My name's Emma, and I'm a sophomore here majoring in chemistry. I love to read, especially Jane Austen novels. Now, I would like to share with you one of my favorite pieces of scripture. I'm usually a King James Version kind of girl, but I think the English Standard Version is easier to understand. If you all will open your Bibles, or pull up your Bible app, to Romans 8:26–27, the verses are as follows:

'Likewise, the Spirit helps us in our weakness. For we do not know what to pray for as we ought, but the Spirit himself intercedes for us with groanings too deep for words. And he who searches hearts knows what is the mind of the Spirit, because the Spirit intercedes for the saints according to the will of God.'

"Guys, how powerful and comforting are these verses? When we are so down, so weak, so desperate, the Holy Spirit intercedes for us. I mean, that's simply amazing." Emma's face was radiant as she spoke. She could feel the Spirit moving through her, giving the words to speak.

Throughout the rest of the night, Emma felt the Spirit moving. God's presence was with them through the wonderful music and the powerful message of compassion. When she rose at the end, before the benediction, she was still filled.

"Before you go for the evening, we would like to thank you again for coming, and we hope you had a blessed time. If any of you feel called to become part of our team, just stick around afterward and we'll talk. Benjamin, could you give the benediction?" Emma asked, stepping to the side.

"Of course," the college chaplain who headed the program spoke as he rose. "May the Lord bless you and keep you in everything you do this week. Peace be with you, brothers and sisters."

As the crowd dispersed, Emma was surprised to see how many students had stayed behind. There were at least a dozen standing in her midst. Her two coleaders, as well as the worship team, joined her. Sebastian, one of the leads, introduced himself, followed by the other, Tasha.

The students were thanked for staying to hear more about the program. Tasks for both setup and cleanup were given, as well as planning each service. The group nodded their heads solemnly, but their faces gave away their excitement at the opportunity to help.

"Emma will be passing around a sign-up sheet," Sebastian said. "Please include your name, phone number, and student email address. We'll reach out to you to give you the details for our next meeting."

As the clipboard was passed around, Emma noticed that Brittany had joined the crowd. She gave her a sweet smile of encouragement, which was reciprocated.

A few of the students stayed behind to help with cleanup, which was much appreciated. As Emma was stacking the final chair to put away, she heard a familiar voice.

"If you're still accepting volunteers, I'd like to sign up," Nicholas said, smiling.

"Really?" Emma asked, reaching for the clipboard. "That's awesome."

"I just felt a real calling, you know? Deep in my soul, I knew that I needed to join the team. God has a reason for putting the desire in my heart."

"He has a reason for everything, and in time, you'll know."

5

After campus worship, Nicholas insisted on walking Emma back to her dormitory as it was dark and a good distance away.

"You did a great job tonight, and you seemed so…confident of yourself." Nicholas looked at her and smiled.

"Well, you can thank the Holy Spirit for that burst of confidence," Emma replied, smiling back. "You can't even imagine how nervous I was beforehand."

"Oh, yes, I can. I saw that expression on your face. One of pure terror. I had the same look on my face when I was told that I would be moving back to England. I didn't know what I was going to do."

"But you did all right," Emma said with encouragement.

"I suppose so, but I really missed us."

"I missed us too," Emma whispered so low that she wasn't sure if Nicholas heard.

As the two reached the front step to Emma's dormitory, Nicholas gently reached down, brought Emma's hand up to his lips, and brushed a gentle kiss across it. Before Emma could say anything, Nicholas was already out of hearing distance.

She opened up her door, walked inside, and leaned against the wall. Emma silently replayed what had just happened and shook her head. No, she couldn't dwell on it. If she did, it would drive her crazy.

She walked into the room and looked around. "Angela?" she hollered out.

"Under the bed," she yelled back. "I dropped something. Oh, here it is." She crawled out, holding a tiny earring. "So how was the service tonight and the part where you had to speak? I know that you were really nervous about that."

"Everything was simply wonderful! Even standing in front of everyone and speaking was amazing. It was as if I was just a vessel that God was using to speak through. You could really feel the Spirit moving tonight! And you would not believe how many students volunteered to help." She held up the clipboard, which Angela took and examined.

Her eyes focused on the bottom name. "Quite an impressive list," she said with approval. "Plus, look who signed up. Your 'friend' Nicholas."

"Angela, Nicholas signed up because he felt led to, that's all. End of story. I promise, no electricity tonight—"

"What do you mean tonight?" Angela interrupted.

"Oh boy, I've said too much." Emma quickly turned around, but Angela spun her back toward her.

"Oh boy, you've not said enough. Spill!"

"Well, you know the other day when you walked in on us staring at each other?"

"Yeah."

"Our hands had kind of brushed beforehand and had lingered a bit. I guess I felt electricity now that I think about it, but I have no idea how he felt. There's nothing to it anyway. He's my friend and will always be my friend. That's all."

"Well, when I walked in on you two, I saw *the look*. Not just from him, but from you too, girl."

"It must have been *a* look, not *the* look."

"You admitted to experiencing electricity the other day, so why not admit to experiencing the look of longing I saw on both of your faces."

"Angela, please, I'm tired. Can we talk about this in the morning?"

Angela was quiet for a few moments. When she did break the silence, she simply suggested that the two go to bed after a long day. She was aware that Emma clearly no longer wanted to speak on the subject but knew that she would dwell on it until she fell asleep.

Dwell on Nicholas that night Emma did. She wanted to have feelings for him but she couldn't. What if he rejected her? Such a sweet friendship could be lost. Besides, there were much more attractive girls on campus that he would be interested in who were far more talented than she was. Emma was just Emma, nothing more. She had believed this since one of her closest friends became angry last year and dubbed her as being less than ordinary. She yelled at her harshly that there was nothing special about her. That she was worthless and would never be loved. Then, she had stopped speaking to her altogether. This girl, Cassandra, had been like a sister to Emma. The two had become friends as soon as they met during freshman year orientation.

Emma had no idea what she had done wrong and had apologized to her to no avail, no comment, simply silence. Their friend group had been split, and Emma had been replaced by a more outgoing, charismatic friend, Katrina, who Emma had also apologized to. Katrina had explained to Emma that both she and Cassandra had not been too fond of Emma's new attitude last year after winter break. She was too confident in herself and needed to be put back in her place. The only thing Emma had done was learning how not to be a doormat and how to stand up for herself. However, she still apologized for this in the presence of both Katrina and Cassandra. The former accepted the unnecessary apology, but the latter had remained silent. Despite Katrina's request, Cassandra acted as if she had heard nothing. This horrible memory is what Emma fell asleep to.

When Emma awoke the next morning, she felt as if she hadn't slept at all. She had tossed and turned, dreaming of Cassandra, worried about their next encounter, praying that she had switched schools. Unfortunately, Emma's nightmare became reality as she ran into Cassandra and Katrina at the cafeteria that evening for dinner.

As Emma was standing in line, she noticed the two sitting in their usual spot, one previously of fond memories now turned dark. They stared at Emma and whispered to each other. When they noticed that Emma was watching, Katrina gave a small yet sincere smile, which Emma reciprocated. Cassandra, on the other hand, snubbed her nose into the air. Emma could feel the tension, and this made her too sick to eat. She immediately left the cafeteria and headed to the gym to refocus and clear her mind.

As she walked into the room full of workout equipment, she smelled the combination of sweat and the metal of the machines. She took hold of her favorite elliptical and began her workout. As her legs began to burn in a satisfying way, she recalled some of her earliest memories of Cassandra—studying together in the library, going to campus worship, night trips to grab doughnuts. Everything had been perfect. The two girls had been inseparable, evening falling asleep while talking to each other. That had all changed now since Emma had the audacity to think of herself for once and grow in confidence. Did she miss her friendship? Dearly. Did she regret what she had done? Absolutely not. There comes a time in everyone's life when you must decide who is writing your story. Emma had taken hold of the pen, and there was no turning back. She would no longer be a doormat but would be her own person.

As she pondered on this, she felt the sweat trickle from her hair down toward her mouth. The salty liquid stopped at her lips. She reached for her water bottle and tasted sweet relief from the cold water.

A few minutes later, Angela walked through the doors and stopped at Emma's station. "What do you think you're doing, Em? I didn't see you at the cafeteria, so I'm pretty sure you haven't eaten. You know that you can't exercise like this!"

Emma remained silent.

"Come on," Angela pleaded. "Let's go grab you something to eat."

"Fine," Emma finally said in defeat.

As she dismounted from the machine, her vision blackened, and she grabbed the elliptical for support. The episode had only lasted a few seconds but was enough time for Angela to take notice. She grabbed Emma's arm as she swayed.

"Are you okay, Emma?" Her voice was full of concern.

"Yeah, this kind of thing happens all the time. My sugar might just be a little low."

"Emma, that's not normal."

"I'm okay. I promise."

"All right. Let me text Sara, and we'll head to a restaurant. Your favorite restaurant."

"Why? I'm really not hungry."

"Because you do need to eat, and we all need to talk."

After picking Sara up, the girls headed to Wing Palace. They placed their orders for the best wings in town and began to talk about what happened with Emma earlier.

"Why were you in the gym?" Sara asked.

Emma looked down. "I saw Cassandra and Katrina."

Angela took Emma's hand. "You can't let them get to you. They're just jealous of how awesome we all are and how far we've come."

"It's just...I know it sounds silly to say because of everything that's happened, but I miss them and that friendship terribly. I understand now that it was toxic, but I don't know. It sounds so ridiculous."

Sara took Emma's other hand. "It's not ridiculous; I understand. The same situation happened to me in high school, and sometimes, I still feel an ache in my heart. But you need a healthier way to cope instead of not eating and heading to the gym. That's dangerous, Em."

"I know. I just couldn't handle being in the same room today." She looked down yet again, and a tear silently rolled down her cheek. "I just don't understand, I suppose. When I finally find my voice, why do people start leaving me?"

"They know that they can't control you," Sara said. "And it terrifies them to think what you are capable of doing on your own."

"Plus, true friends never leave you. They rejoice with you when your confidence rises. We will never leave you," Angela stated.

Emma slowly raised her head to look at her two friends. With eyes glistening, she said, "Thank you both for everything. For being my closest friends and for always being here for me. I don't know what I would ever do without you."

This tender moment passed among the girls, and Emma was not sure what the next day would bring, but she did know that these girls would be with her forever.

6

"Today, class, we will be discussing the laws of thermodynamics," Professor Salyers announced. "These are essential to your coursework and will be on your chemistry oral exam senior year, so go ahead and grab a pencil and paper. We'll dive right in. Does anyone know the first law?"

"The law of conservation of energy," Angela said proudly.

"That's right," Professor Salyers said, a little surprised. "And what does it say?"

"No idea. I just know that because I glanced at the book."

The professor chuckled. "The first law states that energy can neither be created nor destroyed. It can only be transferred or changed from one form to another. The chemical energy we take in while eating is transferred to kinetic energy, which helps us move. Now, does anyone know the second law?"

All eyes turned toward Angela. "Not this time, guys," she said. "Someone else can have a go."

"Entropy always increases," Emma said.

"That's right. Entropy of an isolated system is always increasing. Think about it as a room. If you don't clean it every day, then the dust piles on, and the room becomes more and more disorganized. Even though the entropy inside the room decreases when clean, the effort you put into cleaning it increases the entropy outside of the room. Now for the third law. Anyone?"

"Something about absolute zero," a student yelled out.

"Yes, the third law of thermodynamics states that as the temperature of a system approaches absolute zero, its entropy becomes constant. This means the change in entropy is zero. I know that this is a lot to process, so we'll work on some examples for the rest of the class period."

After the class came to a close, Emma found Angela. "Oh my goodness. I know that it was only one topic, but there was so much information!" Emma exclaimed. "I might as well just go ahead and set up in a room downstairs for the evening."

"Yeah, I'll join you," Angela agreed.

The two girls made their way into an empty classroom due to their usual study area already being occupied by students. Emma and Angela laid out their textbooks, opened their laptops, and began to work.

"My laptop has to update again. Seriously?" Angela said, exasperated. "Well, I might as well do something interesting while I wait." A devilish grin crossed her face. "Let's finish that conversation about you, Nicholas, and the fireworks."

"Let's not."

"Come on, Em."

"Right now? I mean, there's nothing to tell."

Angela arched an eyebrow. "There's nothing to tell about that almost kiss?"

"What almost kiss?" Emma asked in shock.

"If I wouldn't have walked in when I did, I bet I would have walked in on a kiss."

Emma swatted at Angela, who simply rolled her eyes.

"You can't tell me you've never imagined…"

"Imagined what?" This time, Emma's tone was stern, and it was her turn to arch an eyebrow.

"Someone taking you in his arms and giving you the most passionate of all kisses. For you, it's definitely Nicholas; and if I asked him, I'm sure he wouldn't mind." Angela laughed.

"Ang! I've never thought about us like that, and you know it."

Angela didn't seem too convinced by the statement, but she did remain silent.

A few minutes later, the door opened to reveal Sara, Gerald, Thomas, and Nicholas.

"I'm glad we found you both," Sara said. "There's an epic party happening on the other side of campus at one of the fraternities, and we absolutely have to attend! Everyone who's anyone is going to be there."

"I'm in!" Angela said, jumping out of her chair. "You know that I'm always down for a party. Let's go, Em!" Angela began to speedily pack her belongings.

"Sorry, I can't go," Emma replied. "I'm just now starting my physical chemistry homework, plus I have an argumentative essay to begin writing. I'm utterly swamped."

"Please," Sara begged. "We're all going, and it won't be the same without you." She gave a pout.

Emma had mixed feelings about the party. Her extroverted side did want to go, but her introverted side, the dominant side, the voice of reason, decided that it would be better for her to stay. Even though Nicholas would be going, she knew that she had too much work that needed to be completed, and she definitely needed the time to focus on her studies. She politely declined the invitation again.

"All right," Sara said reluctantly.

Emma waved goodbye to the group as they headed off, but a few minutes later, the door opened again.

"Angela, I said that I couldn't come," Emma said, determined.

"Thought you might want a study buddy," Nicholas said, entering the room. "Will I be bothering you?"

"Sorry," Emma apologized. "Of course, be my guest. Maybe with your help, I won't fall asleep."

"Don't worry; you can count on me," he said, smiling.

Nicholas emptied his backpack and took a seat directly beside Emma. She remembered what happened the last time the two were left alone to study together and the conversation she had previously had with Angela about kissing. She blushed and hoped that Nicholas did not take notice. She was close enough to smell the woodsy scent of his cologne. Their knees were almost touching, but not quite. Emma had to muster all of her strength to focus on her homework instead of the beating of her heart. She was able to answer the first few questions about thermodynamics and performed the math accordingly. However, she came to a halt at question number five. She read the question half a dozen times and worked the problem just as many. For the life of her, she just couldn't solve the problem. Nicholas must have noticed her struggle because she was asked if she needed assistance. Emma gratefully obliged and passed her paper over. She looked at him as he stared intensely at the question and her work. He eventually smiled.

"Here," he said, showing Emma the paper. "This negative sign needs to be a positive."

She looked at the problem, confusion clouding her face. "Why? Where does it change?"

"The sign needed to be positive from the beginning of the problem. I know that these laws aren't the easiest to understand."

"Thank you," Emma said, reaching for her paper.

This time, their fingers didn't brush. Instead, their arms, sides, pretty much half of their bodies, leaned against the other. She felt her heart skip a beat, and she had the strongest urge to lean in closer. However, her rational side told her that it wouldn't be the brightest idea on her part, especially since she would then be close enough for a kiss. Perhaps, a kiss wouldn't ruin their relationship... Wait, what was she even thinking? Of course she couldn't just lean over and give him a kiss. Instead, she made herself start to pull back.

Nicholas, on the other hand, took advantage of the brief moment to give Emma a lingering side hug. His embrace was so tender and so warm. Being in Nicholas's arms made Emma feel at home. Now, this was driving her crazy.

Finally, the hug came to an end, and Emma was able to slow her heartrate. The two, however, remained close the rest of the evening, every now and then brushing elbows or feet. Even though there was still electricity surrounding the two, Emma felt a peace about her and was able to accomplish more work than she had thought possible, especially being this close to Nicholas.

"Do you want to grab something to eat?" he asked.

"That would be amazing. I'm famished," Emma replied, her stomach almost growling. "By the way," she began, "how do you know so much about thermodynamics?"

"My father taught me some when I was younger. Plus, I've always enjoyed solving problems. I guess you could say that it's a hobby of mine."

"Hmm…perhaps, then, you could tutor me sometime."

Nicholas's eyes sparkled. "Of course," he said, smiling.

The two finished packing up their belongings, and as Emma did so, she wondered what would happen the rest of the night. She was thrilled, secretly, to be going anywhere with Nicholas, but she reminded herself, time and time again, that they were only friends and nothing more.

7

Emma and Nicholas slowly crossed the campus on their way to the cafeteria. While walking, he took her arm in his like he used to when they were younger. Emma thought that it must be something he learned in England and thought nothing of it; she was simply glad to have him close.

"Emma," he said quietly, "what do you think the meaning of all this is?" He gestured at the campus.

"What do you mean?" she asked.

"I guess I mean, me just so happening to choose the same school that you are enrolled in. I had no clue where you were even at. You don't post on social media too much, so I naturally thought you had chosen somewhere closer to home. What are the odds of us meeting again?"

"I believe that the Lord wants to rekindle our friendship. I think…that we strengthen each other and could do anything together."

"I think that as well," he agreed, stepping back to look her in the eyes. "Let's make a promise right now that we will always be there for each other no matter what. I need you in my life, Em. I couldn't bare it if we drifted away again. God brought us back together for a reason. Let's keep it that way." He put out his hand for Emma to shake.

She grabbed his hand, and he pulled her a bit closer. Instead of shaking her hand, he looked down and gently caressed it with his thumb. Emma looked at him, really looked at him. This was the boy she had grown up with, the boy who had always been there for her. Did she really have feelings for him? Yes, undeniably. Were they reciprocated? She had no clue whatsoever. She and Nicholas had always acted like this, and nothing had become of it previously, so why would this be any different?

As Nicholas lifted his head, he gazed into her eyes yet again. Emma felt herself move closer and closer to him, and she felt Nicholas do the same. Their lips were inches apart. If she moved just a tad closer, she could close the distance, but of course, she couldn't. She couldn't risk their friendship.

"We better be on our way," Nicholas said in barely a whisper. This time, he was the one who broke the gaze. He took her arm again, and the two proceeded to the cafeteria.

After obtaining their dinner, Emma and Nicholas headed to a secluded spot near the windows.

"Nicholas?" Emma asked cautiously. "You said earlier that you had no idea where I was attending school. If you would have known..."

"Yes?" Nicholas motioned for her to continue.

"If you would have known, would you have based your decision on that?" She blushed slightly.

Nicholas looked down, avoiding eye contact. Emma thought that his face seemed redder than usual.

"Sorry," Emma said, a tad flustered. "I shouldn't have asked."

"No, no, it's okay. The truth is that I was praying—have been for a long time—that we would meet again. I was thrilled when I saw you that day at the party. I was just so thankful that God answered my prayer with a yes." He finally raised his head and smiled gently.

"I know that I've missed spending time with you. Not too many students here are fond of any deep, theological conversations. Every once in a while, I can get Angela involved in one, but it's rare and really not the same."

"I understand that. My friends in England are always wanting to talk about anything other than God."

"You mean, they don't believe in Him?"

"Some do and some don't, but you wouldn't be able to tell the difference. They try to involve me in what I consider immoral activities, such as excessive drinking and gambling. When I won't partake in their activities, they tend to make fun of me."

"Well, your friends don't really sound like friends, then. Do they?"

"No, I suppose not. Not like you anyway."

A few moments of silence passed.

"How's your family?" Nicholas asked. "Is your grandfather still working on his divinity classes?"

Emma was secretly glad for the subject change. "He sure is. I think this semester is focused more on the New Testament, leaning more toward Revelation."

Emma was extremely proud of her grandfather. He was a full-time contractor who took classes part-time at the local Bible college. Emma's papaw was her best friend in the entire world, and it just so happened that he would graduate from college the same year as she would.

"Revelation?" Nicholas pondered. "That is an interesting read."

"I know that one Sunday he filled in for our pastor and spoke on the subject. He gave a new perspective on it. Instead of preaching on fire and brimstone, he simply spoke about heaven. So many souls were saved that night."

"What do you think about heaven, Em?"

Emma was taken off guard for a second, but she quickly recovered. "Well, the Bible says that it will be a beautiful place where we will worship God for all eternity. I think it's a place of rest with no sorrow, suffering, or tears. It will be an amazing place to be because that's where God is."

"Do you think that people in heaven can see what we're doing?"

"We won't really know until we're there, but I personally don't think that they can look down on us. The world is full of too much pain, and there is no sadness in heaven."

"Sometimes, when the world around me is more troubling than normal, I close my eyes and just think about what it will be like, surrounded by family members I never even knew, being able to speak with Moses and Paul, finally seeing Jesus face-to-face. It's overwhelming, in a good way, of course. It's relaxing and puts me at perfect peace. Does that make any kind of sense?"

"Yes, I think so," Emma responded. "Especially the part about being both overwhelmed and relaxed. On the surface, or to someone who does not yet know Christ, it may seem like an oxymoron. It's like being overwhelmed with joy and peace. I know that I do the same thing, especially if I become anxious in day-to-day activities."

"I'm glad that I found someone who can finally relate." Nicholas gave a sigh of relief. "Sometimes, I think I'm going crazy."

"If it makes you feel any better, I sometimes stare at the ceiling and ask God what He is doing with my life and what I need to do. I talk aloud to Him, praying for an audible response."

"Have you ever received one?" He leaned in a bit closer.

"Not aloud, but I can feel His presence deep in my soul, in my heart. It's somehow really hard to discern what God wants me to do. I'm always afraid of messing up," Emma said with a slight smile. "But I know that God has a plan for me, and that all things work together for good, just like the Bible says."

The two sat for a few moments, quietly picking at their food.

"This is nice," Nicholas whispered. "It gives me a feeling of being home."

"I feel the same way, such a deep yet peaceful topic to discuss."

Nicholas shyly grinned. "I mean—"

Unfortunately, Nicholas was unable to finish his statement as the couple was interrupted by their group of friends back from the party.

"You two really didn't miss too much," Angela said, sitting down. "Bad music and bad food. I'm famished." She took one of Emma's fries. "So what have you two been up to?"

"The usual," Nicholas said casually. "But I better go. I have some more homework to finish tonight."

"Same here. We'll walk with you," Thomas said, motioning for Gerald.

After the boys were far out of hearing distance, Angela dramatically leaned across the table. "The usual? Does that mean staring into each other's eyes like star-crossed lovers?"

Emma blushed. "Ang, you know very well what he meant." She decided to keep the almost kiss to herself because she would never hear the end of it if Angela found out.

"No, Em, I really don't. It's just always some subtle romantic thing with you two that you don't pick up on. For all I know, he could have been flirting with you all night, and you wouldn't tell me."

"Flirting? One, like I've told you numerous times, I don't know how to flirt. Two, why would he want to flirt with me?"

"Emma, you think too little of yourself," Sara said kindly. "You're a special person who deserves someone special. And maybe," she giggled, "that special someone was just here."

Emma swatted at her. "Not you too!" she moaned.

"So let's get back to business," Angela said. "If you weren't gazing into Nicholas's eyes and you don't think you two were flirting, what exactly were you doing?"

"Just talking."

"About?"

"My goodness! You guys don't need a play-by-play. Next time, don't go to the party, and you can see for yourself."

Angela and Sara looked at each other and then at Emma, who was attempting a stern look. The three girls simply broke into laughter and enjoyed the rest of the night.

8

That weekend, Emma decided to jump into her car and head home for a surprise visit. Even though she still had work that needed to be completed, she missed her family more. She was determined to spend some quality family time during the day and complete her school assignments at night. Plus, she needed a distraction from Nicholas.

Emma's home was only an hour away from the school, but the two could not feel more apart. At school, there were few people she could show her true feelings to, such as Angela. At home, she could just be herself and not worry about putting on a mask. She was so blessed to have such wonderful parents, grandparents, and siblings. They were always there for her no matter what, especially her papaw.

As she pulled up to her modest country home, her younger sister, Lucy, ran up to her.

"Emma! What are you doing here? Never mind, it doesn't matter. I'm just so glad to see you!" Lucy pulled Emma in for a tight embrace.

"Not so tight, Lucy," Emma laughed as Lucy lessened her grip. "I'm glad to see you as well."

Even though Emma's sister was only eleven years old, she was very mature for her age. She helped with cooking and cleaning without being asked, and her homework was always finished in a timely manner. Although she was quite younger, the two had become very close, always confiding in the other, knowing that their secrets were safe.

"Well, Emma, let's grab your bags and head inside."

Emma's fifteen-year-old brother, Jackson, was waiting to open the front door.

"Emma! What a surprise!" he said enthusiastically.

"Hey, Jackson. How have you been doing?" Emma asked.

"Good. I've been making lists about the top ten superheroes and the top ten wrestlers. I have so many to share with you."

"I'm looking forward to it."

Jackson had been diagnosed as having autism when he was younger. Making lists of anything and everything was part of his coping mechanisms. Last year, for Christmas, Emma had made him special binders for his plethora of lists. He had already completely filled three of the binders, and the fourth was halfway full. Emma made a mental note to make him some more.

"Where's Mom and Dad?" Emma asked.

"They headed to the store to grab food for dinner. They're going to be so thrilled to see you here!" Lucy said.

Almost as soon as this was spoken, Emma's parents pulled into the driveway. Her mother was the first to jump out of the vehicle, and she almost tripped running up to her. She threw her arms around Emma.

"Emma," she cried, "I am so happy you are here. Have you eaten today? No? Well then, you must be famished."

"I could eat," Emma managed to say before her father pulled her in for a hug. "Hey, Dad. How's it going?"

"Better now that you're here," he said. "Our family is all together, and that's what matters. Your grandparents are on their way over as well."

Emma's parents, Veronica and Hunter, had the perfect love story. They were high school sweethearts who attended the same college. The last day of classes, her father had taken her mother to the chapel, dropped to one knee, and proposed. Two years after a blissful marriage, Emma had been born. As the family grew, the love grew. The Lewis family was one of the closest families in the neighborhood.

As far as her grandparents were concerned, Barbara and Beecher had also met at a young age. Her grandmother had previously been married and had custody of Veronica. One day, while driving, her fuel was low, so she stopped to buy gas. The man who pumped the gas turned out to be her soon-to-be husband. Her grandfather told the story that her grandmother would buy a small amount of gas, drive around town, and then come back for more. She did this until Beecher had formally asked to court her. Although her grandmother denied this, Emma's grandfather was too convincing. No matter how many times she had heard this, Emma always chuckled at the story.

After Emma had finished unpacking her bags, she headed downstairs for dinner. Upon her arrival, she found that her grandparents were finally in attendance.

"Mamaw, Papaw," she exclaimed, running up to them. "I'm so happy that you're here. It just wouldn't be the same without you."

"Come here," Emma's grandfather said, pulling her in for a bear hug. As he did so, Emma's grandmother patted her head.

"We've missed you so much already," her grandmother said.

"I've missed everyone here too," Emma said. "I'm just so happy to be home for the weekend."

As the family sat down to the dinner table, Emma's grandfather stood up to pray. "Father," he began. "We thank You for this day You have given to us, and we pray that we wake tomorrow to another beautiful day. We ask that You bless this food for the nourishment of our bodies and that You bless the hands that prepared it. We also thank You for Emma's safe journey home and ask that You bless her in all that she does. We thank You, Father, for all the blessings You have given to us. We know that we don't deserve them. Please, forgive us of our sins, and cleanse us from all unrighteousness. Please speak through us, and let us be lights in the community. In Your holy name, we pray. Amen."

The food that evening was spectacular, as always. Her parents truly had a gift in the kitchen, and when they worked together, the gift was always stronger. Emma's grandmother had brought her famous banana pudding, which was the perfect ending to a perfect meal.

After dinner had finished and the dishes were washed, the group moved to the family room. Emma immediately sat down close to her grandfather, who was playing a hymn on the piano. He rarely sung, but he always played the piano or his guitar. When the song came to a close, Emma asked him about what he was learning right now at school.

"Well, Emma," he began, "We haven't quite reached Revelation yet. We are currently studying the Fruits of the Spirit. Would you like to help me study?" Emma nodded her head. "Then, grab your Bible and turn to Galatians 5:22–23. What does it say?"

"The English Standard Version says, 'But the fruit of the Spirit is love, joy, peace, patience, kindness, goodness, faithfulness, gentleness, self-control; against such things there is no law.' You already had that memorized though, didn't you?"

Emma's grandfather laughed. "I did, but I wanted to hear you read it."

"Papaw…" Emma said, chuckling herself.

The more her grandfather laughed, the redder his face became. "Sorry, Emma," he said, wiping a tear from his eye. "All right," he said, composing himself, "now let's talk about what each of these means."

Emma was excited because her grandfather was one of few people whom she could have deep theological conversations. She scooted closer to listen.

"Let's talk about love first," he said. "What is love to you?"

"Well, 1 Corinthians 13 is the love chapter in the Bible. Love is patient and kind. Love rejoices in the truth. You know that."

"Yes, but what is love specifically to you?"

Emma pondered for a few moments. "I suppose that love is safety yet excitement. A feeling of warmth, like the sunshine on your face. Love is the strongest force of all."

"I really like that last statement you made about love being the strongest." Her grandfather smiled. "Let's apply that now to a biblical standpoint. Who in the Bible showed the greatest love?"

"Jesus. He died on the cross for each and every one of us for our sins."

"So are you telling me that He is the epitome of love?"

"Yes," Emma said, smiling ear to ear. "Jesus is exactly that."

"Good. Now, what about joy? What does that mean?"

"Isn't that another word for happiness?" Emma asked.

"That's what people tend to think joy is, but it is far more than simply happiness. Joy is delighting in all circumstances, even the negative ones."

Emma's grandfather was solemn and looked down. He had previously been diagnosed with cancer and was currently undergoing treatment. The chemotherapy had slowly began changing his outward appearance, slightly thinning his hair and making him move slower than usual. However, his mind was as sharp as ever before.

"That's hard to do," Emma said, and her grandfather raised his head.

"I know but it is something that we as Christians need to follow. We need to be examples to the world."

Emma decided to change the topic. "What about peace, Papaw?"

"This chaotic world isn't very peaceful, is it? But the Lord is. He gives us the Spirit of peace, which comforts us, especially in times of trial. Now, Emma, can you tell me about patience?"

"Patience is not something that I'm too fond of, but I've had to be patient so many times and feel like I'm getting better at it. Patience is waiting without complaining."

"What exactly are we waiting on?" Her grandfather was always pushing Emma further and putting her mind to work.

"I know that I'm still waiting on some of my prayers to be answered." She thought of her prayer for her grandfather's healing.

"Good, Emma. Remember as well that we are waiting on the Lord's return to bring us home. We must always be ready and be vigilant in our work of being a good example to others and bringing them to Jesus. Now, kindness and goodness come next. What do you think of those traits?"

"Well, a kind and good person are...well, kind and good."

"Which means?" He encouraged her to continue.

"I can't explain it very well. Aren't those the same as being a nice person, Papaw?"

"Not really, Emma. You could use the words generosity and integrity, but you are right about not being able to explain it too well. Instead, let's talk about integrity."

"That's doing the right thing even when no one is watching."

"Exactly, and doing so for the right reason. What's next?"

"Faithfulness."

"Oh, yes, faithfulness. The Lord is faithful, consistent, and reliable. He is always there for us."

"He's the greatest Friend of all," Emma said.

"He sure is. He wants us to tell Him anything and everything."

"Even though He already knows everything, right?"

Her grandfather gave a nod. "Now, this pairs well with the next: gentleness."

"We want to have a gentle soul, right?"

"Exactly. This is being humble and thinking about others before yourself."

"And even though the Lord is all-powerful, He is also gentle."

"Yes, Emma. There's a reason He's called our heavenly Father. He may chastise us like fathers do, but He also comforts us."

"So the final one is…"

"Self-control."

"I know about that. Self-control is having the strength to say no, but that's hard sometimes."

"It's hard a lot of the time. I know that your grandmother didn't have any self-control when she kept coming back to the gas station," he whispered so she wouldn't hear.

Emma started giggling.

"What's going on over there?" her grandmother asked.

"Biblical talk. Do you all want to join?"

"Maybe another time, dear," she responded.

"So those are the Fruits of the Spirit," Emma said. "I guess I didn't know them as well as I thought I did."

"The important thing is that you are learning. As a Christian, you aren't required to learn everything overnight. Even if you memorize the entire Bible, there will still be things that you don't know."

"Is that why you are taking classes, then? To learn more?" Emma asked with curiosity.

"Absolutely. You are never too old to learn. As long as I'm breathing, I'll keep diving deeper and deeper into the Bible."

That night, Emma thought on her conversation with her grandfather. Was she exuding all of these essential characteristics? If not, where was she lacking, and how could she improve herself? Emma knew for sure that she had to work on her self-control, especially when she was around a certain person.

She pulled out her phone, no missed text messages. She felt a slight unintentional pang in her heart. She shook her head and breathed deeply. Emma had no dreams that night and slept peacefully.

9

Emma arrived back on campus Sunday evening. She had accomplished her goal of both family time and completing her studies and was ready for another week. She had needed the refreshment of being home in order to clear her head. However, in the back of her mind was the oh-so-constant thought of Nicholas. She was still slightly sad that he hadn't bothered to message her any that weekend. Whenever she began to think of him and their almost kiss, she reminded herself about what her grandfather had said about the fruit of self-control. She needed to control her emotions and keep them in check, especially if she wanted to excel at school and stay sane.

"How was your weekend?" Angela asked when she noticed Emma walk in.

"It was exactly what I needed," Emma responded, dropping her bag on her bed. "Anything interesting happen here?"

"No, nothing really. No parties, no fun. Sara came over to the dorm for a bit Saturday, but that's about as interesting as it got."

"You didn't hang out any with the guys?"

Angela arched an eyebrow. "No…why?"

"No reason," Emma said, looking down at her unpacked bag. What she really wanted to know was if she had seen Nicholas any this weekend. She suspected that Angela knew her motive and was surprised that she did not question her further.

The next day consisted of physical chemistry, psychology, and English literature. She hadn't seen Nicholas once and began to wonder if he was okay. She could feel that something was wrong but wasn't quite sure what it was. All she felt was something in her heart.

She had heard someone say before that this was a gift of discernment. She managed to keep her focus in her classes though and on her homework.

After Angela had left the science building, Emma made herself comfortable at her usual table and began to work. As she was in the middle of researching for her upcoming paper, a hand touched her shoulder, and she jumped slightly in her chair.

"Sorry to scare you," Nicholas said apologetically. "Can we talk about something though?"

"Of course," Emma said, looking up from her work. She immediately noticed that his expression was off. "Is everything okay?"

"Yeah," he said, dropping his eyes. "I just wanted to ask your opinion on something."

Emma nodded for him to proceed.

"Gerald and Thomas were encouraging me this weekend to ask Brittany if she would like to go on a date with me." He grabbed the back of his neck with his hand. "What do you think I should do?" He raised his head and locked eyes with Emma.

She gazed for a moment into his intense, deep eyes. Emma could be lost in them forever if she wasn't careful.

She took in Nicholas's full facial expression and noticed that he seemed like a desperate man. All of her being wanted to yell out, "No, she's not the one for you. I am. Choose me." Did he not remember the electricity in the room when their hands brushed? Did he not remember their almost kiss? Maybe she was the only one who felt the electricity. Maybe she only thought that the two almost kissed.

Instead of following her heart, Emma remembered self-control, and the reasonable portion of her brain took over. "You should do whatever you think is best for you," she finally said in a low voice.

"Really, though, what do you think?" His longing eyes looked back into Emma's.

He had given her another chance to voice her opinion, and this time, self-control was much more difficult. Part of her wanted to reach across the table and give him a sweet kiss. As she thought this, their bodies seemed to become closer and closer, almost touching, but not quite.

Even though she did desire to be with him and show her hidden affection, there were far too many variables. What if this completely wrecked their friendship? What if he simply laughed at her and walked away? The only words she could muster to say were, "Brittany seems to be a really nice person, and you two would look good together." Surely, this is what he wanted to hear, so that is what she spoke. She thought later that this had come from her heart. She truly wanted Nicholas to be happy, even if he wasn't with her.

"Okay," he whispered quietly, his face subtly moved closer to hers.

Emma couldn't stand his stare as she was afraid that she would succumb to her feelings. She looked down and began ruffling her papers.

"You're a good friend, Emma," he said, and the word *friend* stung at her heart. "Can I meet you back here later tonight? I might need your help on how to ask Brittany on a date and where we should go."

"Of course," Emma said, attempting a smile. "Just send me a message when you're ready to meet, and I'll head over."

"You're not staying?" he said, and she thought she detected a twinge of sadness in his voice.

"Sorry, I promised Angela that I would meet her at the dorm a few minutes before you walked up," Emma lied. She just couldn't stand to be in the same room as him right now. She felt as if her heart had been torn apart.

"I understand," he said, leaning even closer until their faces were mere centimeters apart. If Emma just moved a bit closer…but no, she couldn't. Instead, she stood up with her belongings and took her leave.

When she arrived at her dorm, she immediately went to her bed and stared at the ceiling due to Angela being gone. As she looked up to the heavens, she whispered, "Why, God? Why?" Emma felt deep in her heart that she no longer had a mere crush on Nicholas. Instead, she felt as if their souls had connected. She had the unconscious feeling that the two were meant to be together. Why, then, had she been unable to share her true feelings with him? She dwelt on this for a while until her swirling thoughts were interrupted by Angela entering the room.

"Oh no," Angela said, rushing to the bed. "I've seen this before from you. What's wrong? Did something happen at home? In your classes? Tell me what's happened."

"Nothing's wrong," Emma lied, sitting up in bed.

"Then why were you staring at the ceiling?" Angela sat down beside her.

"I was just contemplating."

"About what?"

"Well, I promised Nicholas that I would help him, and I'm trying to think of the perfect setting for a date."

"Finally! I've been waiting for him to ask for what seems like an eternity."

"Well—"

"I am so happy for you," she said, hugging Emma. "But I'm surprised that you are the one picking out the spot for you two."

"It's not for us."

Angela paused. "What do you mean?"

"It's for him and…Brittany," Emma finally said, looking down for a moment. "She's a great girl though, so sweet and so kind. The two will be very happy together." She forced a fake smile.

Throughout this, Angela sat in silence, something that she didn't do very often. Emma gently waved her hand in front of Angela's face.

"Earth to Angela. Is everything okay?"

"Is everything okay? Of course not! How could you promise to help Nicholas set up a date for him and another girl?" She was almost yelling at this point.

"You should have seen his eyes, Ang, when he asked if he should even ask her on a date."

"He asked you and you said?"

"I looked at him and told him that he needed to do what made him happy. That answer wasn't good enough for him, so I told him what he wanted to hear. That he and Brittany would be the perfect couple."

Angela smacked a pillow in frustration. "But, Em, how could you do it? I thought there was some chemistry between you two, the electricity, you know."

"I must have imagined it all," Emma said with disappointment in her voice. Her eyes involuntarily filled, and a tear rolled down her face. She quickly wiped it away before Angela could take notice.

"I'm so sorry, Em," Angela finally said.

"There's nothing to be sorry about." Her phone dinged. "Sorry, it's Nicholas. We're meeting in the science building to plan their date." She hung her head slightly. "I'll catch up with you later."

As Emma left her dormitory, she couldn't help but regret what she had failed to say. She took a deep breath and headed to where her *friend* awaited.

10

"So," Nicholas began, "I was thinking that maybe I could take Brittany to see a movie this weekend. What do you think?" He leaned back in his chair with a look of victory on his face.

His demeanor had changed since she last saw him, and he looked the happiest he had yet. She thought to herself that he must be thrilled to be asking the girl of his dreams out and regretted hiding her true feelings. If she would have simply told him the truth, she wouldn't be planning this date right now for him and another girl.

"Hmm..." Emma pondered, grabbing another piece of candy. "No, I don't think so."

"Why not? Is it too cliché? The traditional dinner and a movie date?"

"No, it's just that it's impersonal. The dinner part would work, but during the movie, you'll just sit there. I don't think it would be the best first date."

"Then what are you thinking, Em?"

"I'm not sure. Something where you two can talk and get to know each other better. Maybe a stroll around the park and then dinner?"

"Great," he said with enthusiasm. "Now, what about when I pick her up?"

"What do you mean when you go to pick her up?"

"Well, should I bring flowers, chocolates, or something else?"

"I suppose that most girls like flowers."

"What kind?"

"Roses are supposed to be romantic, so maybe some roses?"

"What kind do you like?"

"Well, me, personally…I prefer carnations. I'm not too fancy."

"Okay, so we have me walking up with flowers, strolling through the park, and then going to dinner. Is that everything?"

"How are you going to ask Brittany?" Emma asked.

"Brittany? I mean, what do you mean about me asking her? Don't I just walk up to her?"

"You could, I suppose. It's direct all right." She giggled.

"What do you want me to do, Em? Ride up on a white horse like her knight in shining armor?" Nicholas began to sound frustrated.

"No," Emma said in a calm tone. "What I mean is that you need to know what you're going to ask. That way, you won't back out at the last minute."

"I guess that makes sense. I'm going to walk up to her, flowers in hand, and ask her, 'Are you free this weekend? If so, would you like to spend this weekend with me?'"

"Good," Emma coached. "But don't ask her if she's free. Just ask if she would like to go on a date. If she's really interested in you, then she'll make the time to see you."

"Okay, but what if she says no?" He gave a slight frown of worry.

"She's not going to say no, Nicholas."

"How do you know? How do you know for sure that she won't say no?" Now, he really seemed worked up.

Emma had no idea what was going on with him. She knew that this date needed to be perfect, but she hadn't realized how much he must have already cared for Brittany. He truly seemed worried that he would be rejected.

"Because…I wouldn't," she ventured and immediately regretted her response. So much for her self-control.

Nicholas's eyebrows raised in surprise as he whipped his head around to stare at her. "Come again?" he asked.

"She won't say no." Emma quickly stood up to take her leave. "Good luck," she said as she rounded the corner.

"Emma!" Nicholas hollered, but she was already gone.

She began panicking. What had she done? Why had she let her feelings slip? Surely she had just wrecked their friendship with a simple slip of the tongue, and she didn't know if she was going to recover from this.

As she reached her bedroom, she began having a full-fledged panic attack. Luckily, Angela was still in the room and had experience with Emma's attacks.

"Sit down here," Angela instructed.

Emma nodded her head and sat down on her bed. She could feel her heart beating so hard that she thought it would jump out of her chest. She took quick, shallow breaths but still felt as if she was suffocating.

"Breathe, Emma. Slow, deep breaths. Yes, that's it. Good job. Now, can you tell me what happened?" she asked gently.

As Emma returned to her normal state, her mind began to unclutter. She sat in silence for a few minutes until Angela prodded her again.

"Well, I think I might like Nicholas."

"And that's what gave you a panic attack?" Angela seemed confused.

"Not precisely," Emma corrected.

"Then what?"

"I might have let it slip that I did like him."

"What? How did he react?"

"I left before he could say anything, but his expression, I can't really tell what it meant. It doesn't matter anyway. We have his date planned with Brittany, and like I said earlier, the two will look good together."

"But wouldn't the two of you look better?" Angela cautiously asked.

"The past is in the past, and I just need to move on. Bury these feelings, you know? I just hope that I can somehow salvage this friendship."

"Emma, you can't run away from what happened, and you can't bury your feelings."

"Why not?"

"It's not healthy, Em. We all have to face difficult emotions in our lives. If you bury them now, then you'll still have to deal with them later."

"Angela…"

"Yes, Em?"

"I…I think that I might be in love, and not that puppy dog kind," Emma finally admitted her feelings to Angela.

At first, she felt relief by speaking them into existence, but this was swiftly followed by a punch to her stomach. Her love was unreciprocated.

"Oh, Emma."

Angela touched Emma lightly on the shoulder as tears began to roll from Emma's eyes. "Why did I do it, Ang? So much for my so-called self-control! It went straight through the window. The worst part is that I can't stop seeing that look on his face. I don't think I've ever seen it before. Oh, Ang, what did I do?"

"You were being human, Em, and I can't believe you kept yourself under control for as long as you did. Whatever happens going forward, just know that I'll be here for you. I always will be." She reached over and pulled her in for an embrace as Emma cried on her shoulder.

"You're such a good friend. I really don't know what I would do without you."

"Well, you won't have to find out. I mean it; whatever you need, I'm your girl."

Emma thought to herself that night that she was so lucky to have a friend like Angela, a friend who would never leave her, one who would always be there for her. There weren't many people in the world who could make this promise and actually keep it. However, she trusted Angela and knew that she would stay true to her word. Even in the horrible instance that Nicholas would choose to leave their friendship, she still had other close friends who would help her through it. She slept peacefully that night, thinking of all of friends and loved ones.

11

The next morning, Emma decided to go to the library's coffee shop instead of the cafeteria for breakfast. She ordered her usual, a raspberry white chocolate mocha with a blueberry scone. As she departed from the library, she noticed that the sunrise was beautiful that morning. It would have been perfect if there wasn't someone walking right in front of it. She couldn't make out the figure, so she continued walking toward the sun on her way to the science building. The mysterious figure happened to be heading in the same direction. Emma squinted her eyes, blinded by the sun, but was finally able to make out the figure—Nicholas. They met at the entrance to the building with the sun still rising.

"Nicholas," Emma spoke quietly at the same time he said her name.

The two smiled, and he motioned for Emma to speak first.

"Good morning. What are you doing here so early?"

"Good morning to you as well. I came to study some before my biology exam."

The tension and awkwardness that Emma had prepared for was nonexistent, as if she hadn't let her feelings slip.

He opened the door for her, and the pair walked inside.

"Beautiful day outside," Emma said.

"Even better view from where I'm standing," he said, looking at Emma, who involuntarily blushed.

"My view isn't too shabby either," Emma playfully said back, and Nicholas grinned.

Emma headed to the first table available and pulled out her laptop.

"What are you working on?" Nicholas asked, leaning close enough to make her heart skip a beat.

"I'm sending out a group email to everyone who was interested in assisting with campus worship. We usually meet on Monday evenings, right before dinner. Do you still want me to include you in it since you're here?"

"I always enjoy receiving messages from you…even though I like seeing you in person much more."

"And why exactly is that?" Emma teased.

"Because," he began with a straight face, "I think I'm in—"

"Hey, Emma," Sara waved her hand, interrupting. "I thought you might like some company this morning, but I see that you already have some." She looked at Nicholas and smiled.

"Good morning. Would you like to join us?" Emma asked.

"Sure," Sara said, plopping down across from Emma and Nicholas. After putting on her headphones and turning on her favorite rock band, she began to pull out her books.

"What were you saying?" Emma asked softly.

Nicholas hesitated. "Biology," he finally said, clearing his throat. "I'm in trouble with this upcoming biology exam."

"Oh," Emma said, a glimpse of disappointment running across her face. "I suppose I'll go ahead and type up this email."

"While you're doing that, I'll begin studying."

"Because you're in trouble."

"Yes, in trouble," he repeated softly, looking at Emma longingly.

Emma once again felt her feelings rush to the surface, but what was she doing? He was supposed to be asking another girl out on a date, and she was supposed to be practicing her self-control. However, she had come to the conclusion that she only had a very small amount when she was around Nicholas. If Sara wasn't sitting right in front of them, she might have leaned a bit closer. His lips were so close. She blushed and chastised herself for even having the thought. Emma turned back to her work, and after a few minutes, Nicholas turned toward his.

As she began to type her email, she quickly began to become distracted by her thoughts. Was he really in trouble with biology or had he wanted to say something else? Too bad Sara had shown up when she did.

While her thoughts were racing, Emma noticed that a certain someone kept sneaking glances at her, and he wasn't too concerned about being caught. She had to force herself to focus on her work. He might be in trouble with biology, but Emma was in trouble with chemistry, specifically the chemistry radiating between her and Nicholas.

When Emma could take no more, she gently closed her laptop and began to pack her bags. Nicholas quickly reached over and took hold of her hand, and she felt the electricity all over again.

"Stay," he barely whispered.

Emma truly did want to stay, but she knew that she couldn't. Although his eyes were pleading, she gently removed her hand, knowing that he would soon be holding someone else's. It would hurt too much to give into her emotions now just to have them torn away later.

"I...I can't, Nicholas," she returned his longing gaze. "I have to go," she said, leaning a bit closer.

As he began to slowly close the gap between them, Emma became aware again of Sara. Nicholas must have thought of this as well due to giving her a quick glance.

"Can I at least walk you out?" His eyes were pleading, as if begging for alone time with her.

"No, it's okay. Good luck on your biology exam."

She finished saying her goodbyes to the two and headed back to her room. Upon arrival, she received a phone call from her mother.

"Good morning," Emma began but was quickly interrupted by a frantic voice.

"Emma! Come home. Now! It's your grandfather. He wasn't feeling well and was taken to the hospital. His cancer has progressed, and he's...he's in the final stages." She began crying loudly on the other side of the phone.

"I'm leaving now," Emma replied numbly and hung up the phone.

She felt as if she was in a daze. Why was this happening, especially to a man who had done so much good in the world? It felt like Emma had just seen him yesterday.

She wrote a quick note to Angela and laid it on her bed before rushing to her car. On the drive to the hospital, Emma recalled all of the conversations that she and her grandfather had. Surely, God would heal him of this illness. Emma prayed harder than she ever had for a miracle all the way to the hospital. She knew deep down that God would provide.

Upon arrival, she met her mother and father in the waiting area.

"Why are you out here?" Emma asked.

"We…we just want to prepare you," her father began as her mother started to weep again. "Your papaw…he doesn't look the same as when you last saw him."

Emma nodded her head with understanding. Mustering all her strength, she followed her parents into her grandfather's room. She stopped in her tracks, understanding what her father had meant. Her grandfather looked like a completely different man. The cancer had completely taken over his body, and he almost looked like a corpse laying there except for the occasional moving of his chest. Emma also noticed her grandmother sitting right next to the bed. Her usual joyful self was now gone, replaced by an ancient grief-stricken woman.

A moan grabbed Emma's attention, and she searched for the source—her grandfather. She almost broke down right then and there but knew that she needed to be strong. The chemotherapy that her grandfather had been taking only now showed its full negative effects. Almost all of his hair had fallen out, and the hair that stayed was paper thin. He had lost so much weight that he resembled a skeleton. Her grandfather's voice was hoarse, and he found speaking more and more difficult. Because of being in the hospital and on the brink of death, he had developed a sickly, pale color.

Emma noticed that he seemed to be drifting in and out of reality. One moment, he was awake and fully conscious, the next moment, he would either be asleep or almost hallucinating. Emma flashed back and remembered how healthy he had previously been, even a month ago. Her grandfather had possessed soft brown hair and a healthy tan from working outside. His musical laugh had been replaced by painful moans.

She slowly walked over to where he lay.

"Papaw…" she began.

"Emma…" This was one of his first responses of the night, and the family members all looked up. "I'm proud of you," he continued before drifting back off to sleep.

She sat down in another chair next to the bed and held on to his hand. Her memories took her back to tender moments that the two had shared together: swinging on the back porch while playing with newly born kittens; eating strawberry short cake, or even better, strawberry funnel cake; all of their long theological discussions. Who else would be there for her like he had always been? God just had to heal him.

Emma was jerked away from her reverie by the calling of her name. She looked around the room and noticed that almost everyone was gone. All that remained was Emma, her mother, and her grandmother. Glancing up at the clock, she noticed that it was late in the evening.

"Emma," her mother said again, "it's getting dark, and we need to get back home to your brother and sister."

"Really?" Emma asked sadly. "Are you sure? Can we stay just a little bit longer?"

"I'm afraid that I can't, but you can stay here with your grandmother if you would like. You look ready to pass out though."

"I suppose I do need a little rest," Emma sighed reluctantly. "I'll come back in a few hours."

Emma stood up and leaned over the bed to where her grandfather could hear her. She expected to receive unintelligible words like her mother had. Tears stained her eyes.

"Hello, Papaw," she gently said.

Her grandfather moved his hand, searching for her. He successfully found it and held on. "Emma," he forced out.

She gave a look of surprise but continued, "I'm heading home for a few hours, but I'll be back as soon as I can. I—" She began to choke on her words. "I love you, Papaw."

Emma saw his mouth open as he tried to form some kind of response. "I love you," he miraculously managed to utter.

She squeezed his hand one last time before she headed out, and she thought she saw a tear roll down his face.

As Emma walked through the front door of her home, Lucy ran up to her and buried her head in her shoulder.

"It's bad, isn't it?" she asked her older sister.

"Yeah." Emma's response was unusual for her as she normally tried to comfort others.

She walked directly to her bed and fell into a deep slumber. Emma was awakened the next morning by her father.

"Get dressed quickly," he yelled out. "Your papaw doesn't have much time left."

While quickly putting on her shoes, Emma heard her parents' voices drift from their room.

"What are we going to do with the children, Hunter? We can't take them with us."

"Veronica, we can take them to the neighbors, but what about Emma? We have to take her."

"She shouldn't have to see that. Seeing someone dead is one thing, but seeing someone dying…no, she just can't see that."

Emma had heard enough. They were planning on leaving her behind, and she was determined not to allow that to happen.

"You're not leaving without me," she almost yelled as she busted through the door. "If you leave me behind, I will never speak to either of you again."

Her parents simply looked at her in disbelief.

"I have to go," she pleaded, tears welling in her eyes. "I need to go. I need to see him again."

After a few minutes and even more arguments, Emma was triumphant. Her mother clearly disapproved, but she did understand.

The family was soon on the road after dropping her siblings off. Emma only hoped that they would arrive at the hospital in time. She began again to pray to God to heal him. He couldn't take her grandfather away from her. He just couldn't.

Emma and her parents quickly arrived at the hospital, and she dashed out of the car as soon as it was parked. She ran through the waiting room to where her grandmother was standing. She turned around to look at Emma, tears drenching her face. "You're too late," she managed to croak out. "He's already gone."

By now, Emma's parents had caught up to her. Her mother turned to her father for comfort, but Emma stood frozen. Her grandfather, her best friend in the whole world, was now gone. She had prayed so hard, so sincerely for him to be healed, for him to survive this horrific disease. Her prayers had failed, and he had died. Maybe she hadn't prayed hard enough.

She tried to find an emotion to convey what she was feeling. Sadness? No, something greater than sadness. Perhaps *anguish* or *torture* would be better words. Emma felt as if her heart had been maliciously torn apart. What was that other feeling though? Disappointment. Disappointment, not in God but in herself. Why had she left to go home? Why hadn't she stayed the night with her grandmother? She was so self-centered, such a selfish human being. She felt a twinge of anger at herself. Almost as suddenly as those emotions appeared, they vanished, leaving her with an emptiness. She would now never hear again his jolly laugh or his convicting voice when he preached the Word of God. She would never again feel the warmth of his bear hugs or the tender kisses on her head.

Emma turned again to look at her grandfather and slowly walked over to the bed, where no one else was. She grabbed his hand like he had grabbed hers the night before, but this time, it fell limply back on the bed. That's when she lost all control. She reached down, hugging on tight to her grandfather as the tears rolled down her eyes. Why? Why had this happened?

She stayed in that mournful position for what felt like hours until someone gently pulled her away. Emma struggled slightly but turned to see that it was her pastor, Andrew Locks. He was a tall older gentleman who usually had a wonderful sense of humor. At that moment, however, humor was far from his mind. His face was grave in the knowledge that he had lost a close friend.

"When?" he asked Emma solemnly.

"Early this morning, before I arrived. I should have stayed. I shouldn't have left. I...I..." The floodgates were wide open now, and Andrew took Emma in his arms.

"It's okay," he said. "It's all going to be okay. Let's all go for a stroll while the nurses do their job."

As he led the family out of the room, he kept a firm grip on Emma in order to keep her from running back to the room. When the group finally reached the hospital chapel, Andrew headed directly to the piano in the corner of the opulent room. As he began to play, Emma fell asleep, trying desperately to forget everything that had happened.

12

After finishing out the week at home, Emma finally returned to school, but she was no longer the same Emma. No, she had experienced undeniable grief; and her heart had been broken, torn, demolished. She couldn't look at herself the same way in the mirror anymore. All she saw was a selfish girl who had chosen rest over her grandfather, especially when he needed her most. She was disgusted with herself. Maybe Cassandra and Katrina had been right all along. This girl didn't deserve to be happy, especially not now, not after everything that had happened.

She was pulled from these negative thoughts by Angela walking into their room. She immediately ran over to Emma and threw her arms around her.

"Emma! I'm so sorry to hear what happened. Do you want to talk about it?"

No, she didn't want to talk about what a despicable human being she was. As she stood motionless, her only reply was, "Not right now, but thank you." She gently pulled away from Angela and began to pack her bag for her first class of the day.

"Are you really going to classes today, Em?" Angela asked with concern.

"Of course, I'm going. Why wouldn't I?" Emma motioned for Angela to follow her out of the room.

Angela quickly grabbed her backpack and headed to the science building with Emma.

"Oh no," Emma said on their walk, "I completely forgot to send out an email about meeting for campus worship. I'll have to see if everyone can meet after classes tomorrow."

"Em…it's understandable that the email wasn't sent," Angela replied back.

"No, it's not." Her expression was fierce. "I'm one of the leaders, and I need to start acting like one. I need to send out that email as soon as we reach the classroom."

Angela remained silent, as if she didn't know what to say.

When the two friends arrived at their chemistry class, Professor Salyers walked up to Emma. "I'm so sorry for your loss, Emma. If you ever need to talk about it, I'm available. In the meantime, there is no rush on your makeup work. You simply take your time and hand it over when ready."

"Thank you, Professor," Emma answered. "But I'll have it done as soon as possible."

He gave her a sympathetic glance and walked back to the front of the room to begin the lecture.

After her classes had finished for the day, Emma stationed herself in one of the classrooms in the science building. She wasn't really in the mood to socialize, so she hadn't revealed her destination to anyone. Pulling out her books and laptop, she began on her missed assignments. The hours flew by to the point that she had missed dinner. She heard a soft knock on the door before its opening.

"Emma? May I come in?" Nicholas asked softly.

"Of course," Emma replied and gestured to the empty classroom.

He walked in cautiously and took the seat closest to her.

"Emma, I heard what happened, and I'm so sorry. I feel deep down, though, in my soul that something else is going on with you. You'll feel much better if you tell me."

"Thank you for your condolences, Nicholas," Emma said in a monotonous voice.

"Em," he said more gently, "tell me…please."

"There's really nothing to tell. He's dead. End of story."

He reached over and gently touched her hand, but Emma flinched away. "I truly am s—"

"Don't," she interrupted.

"Don't what?"

"Don't say again that you're sorry," she said in a louder voice. "Everyone's sorry, but I don't deserve anyone's pity."

"What do you mean by not deserving?"

Her eyelids brimmed with tears. "I—"

"Oh, Em," Nicholas pulled her in for a hug, and she gripped on tight. She felt that if she would let go, she would become lost forever.

She buried her head in his shoulder as he gently stroked her back. Eventually the two broke apart, with him still holding on to her arms.

"If you're not ready to tell me everything, then you don't have to. Just know that I'm here for you when you are."

"I just feel so depressed, all the time, Nicholas. Why? Why did it have to happen? Why did it have to happen to him? He's done so much good in the world, so why did God take him away? I prayed so hard for a miracle, Nicholas, harder than I've ever prayed in my life. God was supposed to heal him." Tears began to slowly slide down her face, and she tried to look away so Nicholas wouldn't see.

"Emma, look at me," he said, but she looked farther away. He reached over and placed a soft hand on her cheek to turn her to look at him. "God did heal your grandfather. He was in pain on this earth, so He brought him to heaven, where there is no pain. God just responded in a different way than you thought He would."

"I can't stop thinking about it."

"About what?"

"All of it. What I did. What I failed to do. Everything."

"What do you mean by failed?" He gave a confused look.

Emma was simply silent. She couldn't talk about this, not now, not ever. She buried her feelings of guilt even deeper inside her.

"I understand," Nicholas said quietly. "We can talk about it when you're ready. In the meantime, though, I think some scripture would really help. Do you remember what you read at the first campus worship?"

Emma nodded her head slowly. Her tears had subsided, and she was now able to speak clearly. "Yes. About the Holy Spirit."

"Exactly. I know you're in pain, Em, undeniably excruciating pain. The good news is that you can talk to God and let Him know how you are feeling."

"He must already know. He must already know the pain that I feel."

"He does, but remember, He wants a relationship with us. If you don't know what to tell Him right now, just give your emotions to the Spirit, and He will translate your feelings into words for you."

"Thank you, Nicholas. Thank you for always being here for me."

"There's nowhere else I'd rather be."

13

Although the weeks passed by quickly for Emma, she still carried her guilt and depression with her wherever she went. She tried on the surface to disguise her feelings, and this worked well most of the time. However, both Angela and Nicholas knew her well enough to know that something else was wrong. They both stayed silent, knowing that she would convey her feelings once ready. The only time Emma did express her emotions was when she would silently cry herself to sleep at night. If Angela had heard her, she didn't comment. Emma had also become more of an introvert, only attending classes and sometimes meals. The rest of her time was spent in her room studying as opposed to the science building.

When the night came for campus worship, Emma simply was not as excited as she had been at the beginning of the year. However, as a leader, she forced herself to attend. She had to set an example to the team. After her grandfather's passing, Sebastian and Tasha had taken over most of the responsibilities, so Emma mainly sat in silence while the team discussed the happenings of the upcoming service. She would occasionally speak when someone asked her opinion on something, whether it be the music for the night or how the room should be set up. To her embarrassment, she had drifted in and out so much during the meeting that she wasn't even sure what the main theme was of the message being delivered that night. She supposed that she would find out eventually.

Instead of her usual spot in the front of the room, Emma took a seat near the back corner. Upon Nicholas's arrival, he took notice and joined her quietly.

"Thank you to everyone for coming tonight," Sebastian announced in a clear tone. "I am so glad to see such a large crowd. I believe this is the largest one so far of the year. If you came just for the pizza and smoothies, then we'll have to make that a regular." He chuckled along with those in attendance. "We really don't have any announcements tonight except for the upcoming hanging of the green. It's one of the most special nights of the year for the campus as a whole, and we hope that you all can attend. Tonight, the message is being delivered by our campus minister, Benjamin."

Benjamin stood and walked over to where Sebastian was standing. Sebastian took a hand and laid it on Benjamin's shoulder before he began to pray, "Father above, we thank You for another beautiful day. We thank You for our campus minister and ask that You speak through him tonight in a mighty way. Open our hearts to receive Your Word. Amen."

"Thank you," Benjamin said as Sebastian headed back to his seat. "Tonight's topic is going to be about forgiveness. Not only forgiving others, not only about God's forgiveness, we are also discussing forgiving ourselves."

Emma's head whipped up. Had she heard what she thought she had?

"Yes, forgiving ourselves," Benjamin repeated, and Emma swore that it was directed toward her. "I know that this can be a difficult topic for some to comprehend, so let's start at the very beginning. John 3:16 says the following, 'For God so loved the world, that he gave his only Son, that whoever believes in him should not perish but have eternal life.' This is one of the most powerful verses in the Bible. God loves us so much that He sent his only Son, Jesus, to save us from our sins. He suffered beatings and tortures. He suffered mocking. He suffered everything for me and for you.

"And then in Luke 23:34, Jesus is on the cross and says, 'Father, forgive them, for they know not what they do.' So here is Jesus, fully man and fully God, asking the Lord above to forgive these people who have tormented Him. He took on the sins of the world—He took on our sins. If you were the only person on this earth, He still would have died on the cross for you. He loves us each that much.

"Now, if Jesus was willing to forgive His persecutors, then why can it be so difficult for us to forgive others? Maybe a friend has lied to you or a significant other has unfairly broken up with you. Have you forgiven them? Colossians 3:13 reads, 'Bearing with one another and, if one has a complaint against another, forgiving each other; as the Lord has forgiven you, so you also must forgive.' This isn't just a suggestion; it's a commandment. Do you know who else you are commanded to forgive? Yourself. If God can forgive you for everything that you've done wrong, then why can't you forgive yourself?

"Tonight, as our worship team plays, I ask that you come forward and write down your sin on a piece of paper. Fold the paper up and nail it to the cross. Let Jesus take away your sin."

Music began to softly fill the worship area, and Emma knew that the Spirit was present. As she walked toward the cross, she felt something or Someone pulling her. She knelt down in front of the cross and wrote down one word: *guilt*. She still felt so guilty that she had left her grandfather, but she knew that she couldn't hold the feeling in forever.

As she began to nail this to the cross, her strength failed her, and she began crying. She felt a strong hand cover hers—it was Nicholas. Together, they nailed her suffering to the cross. He used his strong arms to pull her up and took her to the back corner of the room, where she sunk to the floor.

"Oh, Nicholas," she said, her head in her hands. "I'm so, so..."

"So what, Em?" he asked gently as he stroked her hair.

"Terrible. Selfish. Worthless."

"No, you're not."

"Yes, I am," she corrected. "If you knew what I've done, then you would agree."

"Tell me."

Emma was hesitant but continued, "I...I wasn't with Papaw when he passed. I could have been, but I decided to go home instead. But who does that? Who just leaves someone she loves behind? And for what? A little sleep?" She began to cry harder as she remembered again exactly what she had done.

"Emma, you must have been exhausted. No one can blame you for that, and you can't blame yourself either. Look at me." He gently raised her head and looked her in the eyes. "You have to forgive yourself."

Emma simply shook her head. "I don't know if I can."

"Do you remember us promising that we would always be there for each other? Well, I'm here for you, and we will get through this together."

He took her in his arms again as she cried into his shoulder. The two stayed that way until long after the service had ended. Eventually, she raised her head.

"Do you really mean it?" she finally asked after her crying was close to passing.

"Mean what?"

"That we'll get through this together."

"Every word of it, love."

Her tears ceased, and Nicholas helped her to stand. "Do you feel any better?" he asked.

"I feel like a weight has been lifted off my chest. Like I can finally breathe again. I suppose that I actually do feel better talking about everything instead of burying my emotions. I'm just so used to helping others though. I'm not used to showing my vulnerability."

"Emma, you can't give your help to others if you have no help of your own. I'll be your help. Remember, we talk about anything and everything. You help me with my troubles, and I help you with yours. Ecclesiastes 4:9–10 says, 'Two are better than one, because they have a good reward for their toil. For if they fall, one will lift up his fellow. But woe to him who is alone when he falls and has not another to lift him up!'"

"We are better together, aren't we?"

"We sure are, Em. We sure are."

14

As the week progressed, Emma began to feel more and more like her old self. Gone were her feelings of guilt and shame. She had forgiven herself and no longer believed that she was a horrible, selfish person. Instead, she was someone who deserved happiness and who deserved to be loved.

That weekend, Emma joined her friends for a study party in the science building. They had studied for hours, almost to the point of falling asleep.

"We need to do something," Angela finally announced, standing up. "Something fun to keep us all awake."

"Like what?" Gerald asked.

Her mind began to churn, and she finally looked at both Sara and Emma and gave a mischievous grin. "I was online earlier and ran across a website with the cheesiest Christian pickup lines. Not saying that they're the best in the world, but I think that they would definitely work on me."

"That sounds interesting," Thomas said. "Maybe we should try some out."

"I think I read that same article, Angela," Nicholas said with a sly grin and turned toward Emma. "I was reading in the Book of Numbers last night when I realized that I didn't have yours."

The group laughed in unison.

"Is that how it's going to be?" Emma playfully asked. "Is it hot in here, or is that just the Holy Spirit burning inside of you?" She was rewarded with one of Nicholas's stunning smiles.

"Sara," Gerald said, turning around, "do you believe in predestination? I didn't until I met you."

"The Bible says to greet one another with a holy kiss, so where's mine?" she asked, giggling.

"Right here," he said, walking up to her and placing a kiss on her lips. Her body stiffened for a moment in shock, but she soon recovered. "I've been waiting for a while to do that." Gerald leaned his forehead against Sara's.

"Then, what took you so long?" she asked as the two went in for another kiss.

As they shared their intimate moment, the rest of the group cheered with delight.

"Finally," Nicholas whispered to Emma. "She's all he's been talking about lately."

"It always warms my heart when two people finally find each other," she said.

"Speaking of, Emma," he began, "Can we—"

"Hey, Nicholas," Gerald interrupted, rushing over, "she said that she'd go with me to hanging of the green! How amazing is that?"

"Wonderful, Gerald," he said, smiling. "If you'll just excuse me for a moment—"

"Emma!" Angela yelled out excitedly. "It actually happened."

"I know. I'm so happy for them," she replied back.

Nicholas turned once again to Emma. "We need to—"

"Oh my goodness!" Sara exclaimed to Emma, running over. "Can you believe that happened just now? I don't even know what I'm feeling."

"Maybe you should talk with Gerald," Nicholas suggested. "You two must be feeling the same emotions."

"Of course," she said, placing her hand on her forehead. She immediately walked over to him, and the two headed off down the hallway.

"Emma, we need to talk," Nicholas finally managed to say.

"I'm listening," she said.

"No, I mean we need to talk in private."

"Is everything okay?" she asked with concern evident in her voice.

Nicholas didn't reply. He simply took her hand and led her downstairs.

They stood near the pendulum, one of Emma's favorite parts of the building. She watched it sway back and forth. It was a constant reminder to her to keep moving no matter how bad life became. She visited the place more often now after her grandfather's passing.

"Emma," Nicholas began, "I need to ask you something, and it's okay if you say no."

"What's wrong?" she asked gently. "You look nervous."

"It's just," he said, grabbing the back of his neck, another one of his nervous gestures.

"Just what? Remember, we can tell each other anything."

"Well, I was wondering if…you would like to go with me…to hanging of the green."

"What about Brittany? Shouldn't you be asking her?" A look of confusion flashed across her face.

"No, Em. I'm asking you. Would you like to go with me?"

He searched her face in anticipation, and she noticed that it was the same look he had given her when he had originally asked her for her opinion on asking Brittany on a date. Had he wanted her originally to tell him no? Had he, Nicholas, wanted to be with her from the beginning?

"Yes," she said. Without even thinking, she reached down and took hold of his hand. "I'd love to go with you."

"I'll pick you up tomorrow beforehand." He raised her hand to his lips and gave a soft kiss.

The two looked at each other with longing and began inching ever so closer to each other. Nicholas placed his hand on Emma's waist, and she wrapped her arms around his neck. As they began to lean in for their first long-awaited kiss, they were interrupted by someone trampling down the stairs, and the two quickly jumped apart.

"There you are," Thomas said. "We've been looking everywhere for you two. We're going to pack up for the night and get a fresh start tomorrow."

"We'll be up in just a moment," Nicholas responded with a hint of aggravation, and Thomas quickly took his leave.

As the two headed upstairs, Emma couldn't help but replay that almost kiss. Would it really have happened if Thomas hadn't interrupted them? She wondered what it would be like to kiss someone she truly loved. If electricity sparked when the two were in the same room together, then a kiss like that must be magical.

After she had finished packing her belongings, she gave Nicholas one last longing glance, which he reciprocated. Was he also thinking about what just happened? He gave her a wink, and she immediately knew the answer. As she fell asleep that night, she thought that maybe, just maybe, Angela had been right all along.

15

"Emma, are you almost ready?" Angela asked. "Nicholas is going to be here any moment now."

"I think so," Emma said, emerging from the bathroom. "How do I look?"

Angela was speechless.

"Do I look that bad? I knew I should have just stuck to jeans and a sweatshirt—"

"No, Em. You look absolutely stunning."

"Are you sure?" she asked, picking at her bracelet.

"Turn back to the mirror and take a good look at yourself. Now, what do you see?"

Emma stared intensely at the mirror to the point that she hardly recognized herself. Her hair was perfectly straight instead of pulled back into her comfortable ponytail. She had chosen to wear a green long-sleeved lace dress that hit right past her knee. A pair of high heels accompanied her outfit.

"I see someone that I don't even know."

Angela came to stand behind her and looked in the mirror with her. "You know her, Em. She's a part of you that you just don't see that often. Now, the more important question: Is Nicholas coming here to pick you up, or are you meeting him at the chapel?"

"I think he's coming here, but I'm not 100 percent positive."

"I'm a little surprised that you're not freaking out any." Angela nodded with approval.

"Oh, believe me, I am. I've debated several times about just staying here and feigning illness."

"Nicholas either wouldn't believe you or he would stay with you to nurse you back to health. Staying here is out of the question. You are going. Now just breathe."

As soon as Emma began to take a deep breath, there was a knock at the door. Angela ran to take a quick peek.

"It's him!" she exclaimed a tad too loud for Emma's comfort. He brought flowers!"

"Not so loud, Ang. Besides, maybe I should just stay here." She started to take off a heel.

"Oh, no you don't," Angela said forcefully, pushing Emma toward the door. "I am seeing this love story between the two of you to the end."

Before Emma could get another word in, Angela had already opened the door. Nicholas was standing there awkwardly on the front step, but as soon as he took notice of Emma, all the awkwardness faded away. How could she feel so excited yet so calm being around him?

"I wanted to arrive a little early to surprise you," he said as he handed her a bouquet of carnations.

She felt the heat rise to her cheeks.

"Oh, how thoughtful," Angela interjected, pushing Emma out the door. "I'll take these flowers and put them in a vase for you, Em. Well, you two need to be going, and I need to finish getting ready. I'll meet you in the chapel."

The door slammed shut.

"Well then," Nicholas motioned, "shall we?"

As Emma walked off the front step, she felt the full force of the winter air and felt it burn in her lungs. She had always enjoyed the cool winter weather and was never bothered too much by the cold. However, tonight, the atmosphere was a little warmer than usual due to a certain someone walking right next to her. He took her arm in his, and she felt the electricity all over again. She wondered to herself if Nicholas felt as crazy about her as she was feeling about him. Was he nervous any? What were the plans for the evening?

Emma took notice that they were near the park and then realized something. This was the date that she had helped him plan. He had brought her carnations, her favorite. He had decided to take her to the park, another one of her ideas. She had essentially planned the perfect date, and it had been for her all along.

"So," Nicholas finally broke the silence, "what are you most looking forward to tonight at the hanging of the green?"

Emma thought for a moment. She enjoyed every part of the ceremony, from the singing to the message. However, one part stood out from the rest.

"I love how we all stand outside at the end and light candles. We sing until all of the Christmas lights are turned on, and there's just something so magical about that moment."

"What about the magic you're feeling right now?" He turned and stepped a bit closer to her.

She tilted her head up to look at him. His eyes were so perfect; he was so perfect. This time, she moved closer to him.

"Emma," he began, "the way you speak about things, even as simple as a ceremony…you're always full of passion. Every time I hear you talk, you light a fire inside of me. Never have I ever met someone like that, and I sometimes forget how…"

"How what?" she encouraged him to continue.

"How amazing you are," Nicholas said softly as he stared intensely into Emma's eyes. It was as if he was penetrating her soul, and she stared back into the depths of his.

An eternity seemed to pass. He slowly raised his hand and placed it on her cheek, which she leaned into. The snow began to lightly fall.

"Emma, I think I'm in love with you," he whispered as his face closed the mere inches between the two.

"And I think I've fallen in love with you." She closed her eyes and felt the snow hit her cheeks.

She smelled the sweet aroma of Nicholas's cologne, and suddenly, his lips were on hers. She had longed for this moment, and it was finally reality. Her arms slowly made their way around his neck, and his found the small of her back. After a few moments, the kiss broke, but their foreheads still lay against each other.

"I've been waiting since England to do that," Nicholas said, smiling.

"And I've been waiting to do this," Emma responded, pulling him in to a much more passionate kiss now that the other knew that it was reciprocated.

After a few minutes, Emma's phone dinged; and after the third time, she broke the kiss.

"It's Angela," Emma said, and Nicholas groaned. "She's saving our seats and wants to know where we're at."

"As long as she doesn't want to know what we're doing," he said as he kissed her again; this time, much more slowly.

"Come on," he finally said. "We better be going."

Emma reached up and gave him one more quick kiss. "So what you're saying is that you're not in trouble with biology," Emma chuckled, remembering him trying to tell her earlier.

He simply laughed and pulled her in for another kiss. "No, I'm in trouble because I can't stop thinking of you."

The two walked arm in arm to the chapel and found Angela in the back.

"Sorry, guys, but these were the only seats that I could find. I thought you two would beat me here anyway. Where were you two? Why are your faces getting red?"

"Ang, it's cold outside, so of course, our cheeks are going to be red. Thank you, by the way, for grabbing our seats. We're super excited for the ceremony."

"Of course," Nicholas said, grinning. "Excited...for the ceremony."

"All right then," Angela said, still sounding suspicious.

The three took their seats, and as the lights dimmed, Nicholas absentmindedly took Emma's hand. This felt right to Emma, like she was finally home. She felt so safe around him, and she now knew the reason that God had brought them back together.

A few points during the ceremony, their knees brushed, or Nicholas would play with her feet. Emma had to muster all of strength to stay focused on the message.

After the main service had ended, the speaker, Matthew, encouraged the audience members to each grab a candle to light outside before turning on the Christmas lights. As Emma, Nicholas, and Angela stood, Nicholas offered to grab their candles. He gave a lingering glance at Emma and then headed toward the stage. As soon as he was out of sight, Angela let out a squeal.

"Girl," she said, "there is definitely something going on between the two of you. I could literally see the electricity between you both! Spill!"

Emma simply smiled at her and said, "Something happened that should have happened a long time ago."

"What?"

Emma blushed and looked down. "Let's just say that it was a warmer walk over than I thought it would be."

"Oh my goodness! Did you two—"

At that time, Nicholas returned with the three unlit candles, and Angela silenced herself. He handed Angela's to her, and she swiftly departed. Before passing Emma hers, he gently raised her hand to his lips to brush the most tender of kisses. This was beginning to become a habit of his that Emma definitely did not mind.

The two made their way, hand in hand, outside the chapel to the lampposts. The candles were lit one by one, and all began to sing. As the first chorus was finishing, the campus came to life. The Christmas tree was lit, along with lights wrapping the streetlights. This year was much more magical with Nicholas at her side.

After the singing had subsided, each individual candle was blown out and returned. Nicholas brought Emma closer than she already was and gave her the most tender of kisses. Their lips lingered for a few seconds afterward, and when the two finally broke apart, there was a familiar figure slightly bouncing next to them.

"Thank the good Lord above," Angela yelped. "What a perfect first kiss! I'm so glad that I was here to see it!"

The couple looked at each other, blushed, and then looked down at the ground.

"What? This wasn't your first kiss? How about your first kiss of the night?"

The two were still staring at the ground, but Emma gave a quick glance at Angela before turning toward Nicholas. "Is this kiss number three or four?"

"I'm not sure," he responded. "I kind of stopped counting after you attacked me." Emma blushed. "By the way, feel free to attack me anytime." He winked and gave her a sly grin.

"Lost count? Attacked?" Angela asked. "What did you do, Emma? Finally brave enough to throw yourself at him? That's my girl."

"Actually," Emma corrected, "he threw himself at me first."

"It was mutual," Nicholas said. "And neither of us really seemed to mind. I know that I sure didn't."

"Neither did I," Emma said, turning her head again toward Nicholas.

Before another kiss could ensue, Angela suggested that the three head to the cafeteria for hot chocolate and to warm up. Even though neither Emma nor Nicholas needed warming up at the moment, they still followed her inside and met up with Gerald, Thomas, and Sara.

"Great music, Thomas and Sara," Angela said.

"And great projection from you, Gerald," Nicholas added.

"Thanks. I'm always so nervous when I first get up there to sing," Sara said.

"But you always do a great job," Gerald said, leaning over and giving her a kiss on the cheek. She blushed slightly.

"So, Nicholas," she said, "did you like tonight?"

"He sure did," Angela said, winking.

"I think she meant the service, Ang," Emma replied.

"Why? What else happened tonight?" Sara took notice of Emma's and Nicholas's hands intertwined. "Well, it's about time."

"About time for what, sweetie?" Gerald asked, and she motioned toward the new couple.

"Finally!" Gerald and Thomas said in unison.

"You've only been talking about her since you saw her at the party at the beginning of the semester," Thomas said, laughing.

"And she's only been thinking about him since then," Angela interjected.

"Like I said, it's about time," Sara chimed in.

At that moment, Nicholas twirled Emma around and dipped her, giving her another passionate kiss. As the kiss broke, the group of friends howled with delight.

"Well, Thomas," Angela said, "it looks like we're the only two in the group now who are single."

"Talk about yourself," he said as he walked over to talk with Brittany. She smiled and nodded her head. Upon his return, he said, "See? Asking a girl out on a date isn't that hard. Emma, I hear that you are fantastic at planning dates. Want to help me plan mine?"

She simply laughed and shook her head. "I think I'm done planning dates for now." She noticed Angela scanning the cafeteria. "Ang, what are you doing?"

"Looking for my knight in shining armor, Em. You found yours, and Sara and Brittany found theirs. I think it's my turn."

"You can't rush into love; it just happens naturally."

"Well, I'm sure not going to wait as long as you and Nicholas did. I'm not that patient."

"I didn't think I was either," Nicholas said, smiling at Emma.

"But it was worth it," she said, smiling back. "He was definitely worth waiting for."

About the Author

Author, helper, encourager, seeker of knowledge—these descriptions encompass the essence of Jordan Smith. She began her writing career in high school and was published with the Association of Christian Schools International with the short story "La Promisa." Jordan continued her writing career at Georgetown College, where she was first author in an article for the *Journal of Chemical Education*. After majoring in chemistry and psychology, she took a brief hiatus before continuing with graduate school. Jordan is currently a therapist and case manager, where she advocates strongly for her clients.

CPSIA information can be obtained
at www.ICGtesting.com
Printed in the USA
BVHW082249020921
615904BV00003B/485